First World War
and Army of Occupation
War Diary
France, Belgium and Germany

1 INDIAN CAVALRY DIVISION
Lucknow Cavalry Brigade
29 Lancers
10 August 1914 - 31 December 1916

WO95/1174/3

The Naval & Military Press Ltd
www.nmarchive.com
Published in association with The National Archives

Published by

The Naval & Military Press Ltd

Unit 10 Ridgewood Industrial Park,

Uckfield, East Sussex,

TN22 5QE England

Tel: +44 (0) 1825 749494

www.naval-military-press.com

www.nmarchive.com

This diary has been reprinted in facsimile from the original. Any imperfections are inevitably reproduced and the quality may fall short of modern type and cartographic standards.

© Crown Copyright
Images reproduced by permission of The National Archives, London, England, 2015.

Contents

Document type	Place/Title	Date From	Date To
Heading	WO95/1174/3		
Heading	B E F 1 Ind. Cav. Div. Lucknow Bde 29 Lancers 1914 Aug to 1916 Dec		
Heading	War Diary (1914) From 10/8/14 To 31/10/14		
War Diary	Poona	10/08/1914	12/10/1914
War Diary	Authority Zelegram no 85/15 Simla	12/10/1914	12/10/1914
War Diary	Authority Zelegram no 603 from AHQ Simla	13/10/1914	14/10/1914
War Diary	Bombay Docks S S. Cuts of Baroda	15/10/1914	15/10/1914
War Diary	Bombay Harbour	16/10/1914	16/10/1914
War Diary	S S. City of Baroda	17/10/1914	31/10/1914
Heading	War Diary of 29th Lancers From 1-11-14 To 29-11-14 Volume		
War Diary	City of Baroda	01/11/1914	09/11/1914
War Diary	In Train	10/11/1914	11/11/1914
War Diary	Camp La Source	12/11/1914	14/11/1914
War Diary	Camp La Source Orleans	00/11/1914	00/11/1914
Heading	War Diary of 29th Lancers From 1-11-14 To. 31-12-14 Volume I Pp 26 to 32		
War Diary	City of Baroda	01/11/1914	06/11/1914
War Diary	Camp Borely	07/11/1914	09/11/1914
War Diary	In Train	10/11/1914	11/11/1914
War Diary	Camp La Source	12/11/1914	15/11/1914
War Diary	Camp La Source Orleans	00/11/1914	00/11/1914
Heading	War Diary of 29th Lancers From 6-12-14 To 31.12.14 Volume		
War Diary		06/12/1914	31/12/1914
Heading	War Diary of 29th Lancers. From 1st January 1915 To 29th January 1915		
War Diary		01/01/1915	29/01/1915
Heading	War Diary of 29th Lancers. From 2nd February 1915 To 8th February 1915.		
War Diary		02/02/1915	08/02/1915
Heading	War Diary of 29th Lancers. From 15th February 1915 To 22nd March 1915		
War Diary		15/02/1915	22/03/1915
Heading	War Diary of 29th Lancers. From, 1st April 1915 To, 20 April 1915		
War Diary		01/04/1915	28/04/1915
Heading	War Diary of 29th Lancers. From 1st May 1915 To 31st May 1915		
War Diary		02/05/1915	31/05/1915
Heading	War Diary of 29th Lancers. From 1st June 1915 To 30th June 1915		
War Diary	Vlamertinghe dismounted inst.	01/06/1915	03/06/1915
War Diary	Vlamertinghe	03/06/1915	04/06/1915
War Diary	Ypres	04/06/1915	07/06/1915
War Diary	Vlamertinghe	07/06/1915	30/06/1915
Heading	War Diary of 29th Lancers. From 1st July 1915 To 31 July 1915		
War Diary		01/07/1915	27/07/1915

Heading	War Diary of 29th Lancers. From 1st August 1915, To 31st August 1915			
War Diary			31/07/1915	31/08/1915
War Diary	Fieffes		22/08/1915	22/08/1915
War Diary	Mailly-Maillet		23/08/1915	23/08/1915
War Diary	Authville		24/08/1915	31/08/1915
Heading	War Diary of 29th Lancers. From 1st September 1915 To 30th September 1915			
War Diary	Authville		01/09/1915	03/09/1915
War Diary	Frechencourt		03/09/1915	03/09/1915
War Diary	Montrelet		03/09/1915	03/09/1915
War Diary	Frechencourt		03/09/1915	03/09/1915
War Diary	Senlis		04/09/1915	07/09/1915
War Diary	Frechencourt		12/09/1915	13/09/1915
War Diary	Authville		13/09/1915	14/09/1915
War Diary	Front Line Trenches G. Section		15/09/1915	26/09/1915
Heading	War Diary of 29th Lancers From 1st October 1915 To 31st October 1915			
Miscellaneous	To The Adjutant General L. India Simla		23/11/1915	23/11/1915
War Diary			01/10/1915	31/10/1915
Heading	War Diary of 29th Lancers. From 1st November 1915 To 30th November 1915			
Miscellaneous	To the Adjutant General L. India Simla			
War Diary			01/11/1915	27/11/1915
Heading	War Diary of 29th Lancers From 1st November 1915 To 30th November 1915			
Miscellaneous	Summary of Events and Information			
War Diary			01/11/1915	27/11/1915
Heading	War Diary of 29th Lancers From 1st December 1915 To 31st December 1915			
Miscellaneous	To The Adjutant General L. India Simla.		27/01/1916	27/01/1916
War Diary			01/12/1915	26/01/1916
Miscellaneous	On His Majesty's Service.			
Heading	F.D.O. No. 15			
War Diary			05/02/1916	26/02/1916
War Diary	The Adjutant General L. India Simla		02/04/1916	02/04/1916
War Diary			26/03/1916	26/03/1916
Miscellaneous	Army Form C. 398.			
Heading	The Envelope To Be Returned To Bearer.			
Miscellaneous	To The A.G. in India Simla		03/05/1916	03/05/1916
War Diary			01/04/1916	19/04/1916
Heading	War Diary of 29th Lancers. From 1st May 1916 To 31st May 1916			
War Diary			09/05/1916	24/05/1916
War Diary			02/05/1916	02/05/1916
Miscellaneous	To the Chief of General Staff Simla		01/07/1916	01/07/1916
War Diary			18/06/1916	28/07/1916
War Diary			08/07/1916	08/07/1916
War Diary	Chelers		01/08/1916	07/08/1916
War Diary	Warlincourt-Le-Pas		09/08/1916	21/08/1916
War Diary			20/08/1916	20/08/1916
War Diary	Warluzel		29/08/1916	03/09/1916
War Diary	Outrebois		04/09/1916	04/09/1916
War Diary	Domvast		05/09/1916	10/09/1916
War Diary	Bealcourt		11/09/1916	12/09/1916
War Diary	Milly		13/09/1916	13/09/1916

War Diary	Querrieux	14/09/1916	15/09/1916
War Diary	Dernancourt	16/09/1916	26/09/1916
War Diary	Mametz	27/09/1916	27/09/1916
War Diary	Bussy-Le-Daours	28/09/1916	28/09/1916
War Diary	Hangest-Sur-Somme	29/09/1916	29/09/1916
War Diary	Bellancourt	30/09/1916	30/09/1916
War Diary	Machiel	01/10/1916	02/11/1916
War Diary	Chepy	03/11/1916	31/12/1916

WO 95/11743

BEF

1 IND. CAV. DIV.

LUCKNOW BDE

29 LANCERS

1914 AUG - 1916 DEC

Army Form C. 2118.

WAR DIARY

INTELLIGENCE SUMMARY.
(Erase heading not required.)

Lucknow

Summary of Events and Information.	Remarks and references to Appendices
	12/2168

29th Lancers.

Nº 1-25

Confidential

WAR (1914) DIARY

from 15/8/14
to 31/10/14

Hour, Date, Place.

8 pm. 13/8/14

Instructions regarding War Diaries and Intelligence Summaries are contained in F. S. Regs., Part II, and the Staff Manual respectively. Title pages will be prepared in manuscript.

CONFIDENTIAL.

Army Form C. 2118.

WAR DIARY
—or—
INTELLIGENCE SUMMARY.

of 39th LANCERS.

from AUGUST 10th to October 31st 1914

(Erase heading not required.)

Instructions regarding War Diaries and Intelligence Summaries are contained in F. S. Regs., Part II, and the Staff Manual respectively. Title pages will be prepared in manuscript.

Hour, Date, Place.		Summary of Events and Information.	Remarks and references to Appendices.
1914			
POONA. Aug 10.	5 pm	Telephone message from B.M. to recall BOs on leave in India	QMG's 13 8/14
Aug. 13.	8 pm	Orders received recalling all leave and furlo' men, and calling out all reservists.	4593/3
Aug 14.	11 am	All wires sent.	
	9 am	C & D sqdns medically inspected. Preliminary measures for mobilisation, such as lists of horses for F.S., kits inspected etc. were commenced.	
Aug 15.	9 am	A & B sqdns medically inspected.	
Aug 26	11.30 am	Mobilisation orders received "for possible service with I.E.F. "A"." wired for 64 horses from 27th Lt. Cavalry at Neemuch (with saddlery). Mobilisation commenced — swords & lances re-sharpening and toeplates fixing started	56/9 of 25 8/14

WAR DIARY
INTELLIGENCE SUMMARY.
(Erase heading not required.)

Army Form C. 2118.

Hour, Date, Place.	Summary of Events and Information.	Remarks and references to Appendices.
1914 Poona		
Aug 27th 9 am	1st day of mobilisation. Regt reported medically fit. Reservists medically examined. Regt reported medically fit (3 unfits & 2 absent)	
11 am	Application for 1 NO. 1 NCO, 6 Sikhs & 1 Jat to the 2nd Lancers, Saugor – to make up 10% for 1st Casualties.	
3.30 pm	Veterinary Examination of Regt. Regt reported "fit for service" by Vet. officer. N.B. Reported Rat not probably completed by 31st inst.	
Aug 28th	Lt. Col. J.P.P. Hard. arrived. Wires received from 27th Cav. & 2nd Lancers stating the horses were dispatched by special 28th/14, and Kishan arriving 30th or 31st, and the men arriving 29th inst.	
Aug. 29th	The following officers arrived from England Major Littington, Lt Bacon. Still absent 1 Reservist, 1 Furlo'man	

Army Form C. 2118.

3

WAR DIARY
or
INTELLIGENCE SUMMARY.
(Erase heading not required.)

Instructions regarding War Diaries and Intelligence Summaries are contained in F.S. Regs., Part II, and the Staff Manual respectively. Title pages will be prepared in manuscript.

Hour, Date, Place.	Summary of Events and Information.	Remarks and references to Appendices.
1914 POONA Aug 29th	The following officers now with Regt:— Lt Colonel Hollard (E) Lt Colonel D. Saunders Major Littlingston (E) Capt Meynell Capt Marchant Capt Hemans Capt Henderson (I) Capt Martin Capt Jackson (I) Lt Bacon (E) Lt Wright Lt Bradley (I) Lt Boggs Major Birch expected to-day. 5 Capt Dickson may arrive any day (having resigned his appointment) 5 pm The N.O., NCO, & 11 men from 2nd Lancers arrived	E = from England I = joined in India.

Army Form C. 2118.

WAR DIARY
INTELLIGENCE SUMMARY
(Erase heading not required)

Hour, Date, Place.	Summary of Events and Information.	Remarks and references to Appendices.
1914 Poona Aug 30th	Arrangements made for Depot cmdr, and promotions in case of orders to move. Progress has been reported daily to AQMG Divnl. Hd. Qrs. Lt. Bacon & Lt. Briggs detailed for Depot.	
Aug 31st	64 horses arrived from 27th Lt. Cavalry. Men evacuated open lines & went into tents. Lines cleared for storage.	

Army Form C. 2118.

WAR DIARY

INTELLIGENCE SUMMARY.

(Erase heading not required).

Instructions regarding **War** Diaries and Intelligence Summaries are contained in F. S. Regs., Part II, and the Staff Manual respectively. Title pages will be prepared in manuscript.

Hour, Date, Place.	Summary of Events and Information.	Remarks and references to Appendices.
Poona - 1914 - September 1st		
8 am	Horses from 27th Lt. Cavalry distributed among sqdns.	
10 am	Inspection in F.S order of A & B sqdns.	
5 pm	Inspection in F.S order of C & D sqdns.	

Army Form C. 2118.

6

WAR DIARY
INTELLIGENCE SUMMARY.
(Erase heading not required.)

Instructions regarding War Diaries and Intelligence Summaries are contained in F.S. Regs., Part II, and the Staff Manual respectively. Title pages will be prepared in manuscript.

Hour, Date, Place.	Summary of Events and Information.	Remarks and references to Appendices.
POONA 1914 Sept. 2nd. 7 am	Sqdn inspected in F.S. order.	
9 am	Message sent to Divnl Hd Qrs "Mobilisation completed & Regt. in readiness to move".	
	Sent for 26 more horses from the 27th L. Cav. for reinforcements due to further castings. (This was refused us as they stated in a wire no further horses available).	

Army Form C. 2118.

WAR DIARY
INTELLIGENCE SUMMARY.
(Erase heading not required.)

Instructions regarding War Diaries and Intelligence Summaries are contained in F. S. Regs., Part II, and the Staff Manual respectively. Title pages will be prepared in manuscript.

Hour, Date, Place.	Summary of Events and Information.	Remarks and references to Appendices.
Poona 9th Sept.	Wrote a letter to AQMG for forwarding to AG in India asking for 45 more horses	

Army Form C. 2118.

WAR DIARY
— OF —
INTELLIGENCE SUMMARY.
(Erase heading not required.)

Hour, Date, Place.	Summary of Events and Information.	Remarks and references to Appendices.
Poona 10th Sept.	Wrote letter from Simla (AG) objecting to request for 45 more horses & demanding explanations. Explained that it was to replace greys, Syrolds and camels. Major K.K. Birch returned from Ahmednagar. (He hitherto officiating as Brigade Major)	

Army Form C. 2118.

WAR DIARY
of
INTELLIGENCE SUMMARY.
(Erase heading not required.)

Instructions regarding War Diaries and Intelligence Summaries are contained in F. S. Regs., Part II, and the Staff Manual respectively. Title pages will be prepared in manuscript.

Hour, Date, Place.	Summary of Events and Information.	Remarks and references to Appendices.
11th Sept. Poona.	Capt Dickson reported his arrival in India	

Army Form C. 2118.

10

WAR DIARY
INTELLIGENCE SUMMARY.
(Erase heading not required.)

Hour, Date, Place.	Summary of Events and Information.	Remarks and references to Appendices.
Poona 15.9.14	Increase of one extra blanket for soldiers & followers. Extra flannel shirt, vest & drawers sanctioned for Indian Troops	QMG's wire no 29/58 WS. d. 11.9.14 forwarded by B/M's 395. 14 9/14. QMG's wire no 17/22 WS. d. 11.9.14. by BM's no 396. 14 9/14

Army Form C. 2118.

WAR DIARY
INTELLIGENCE SUMMARY.
(Erase heading not required.)

Instructions regarding War Diaries and Intelligence Summaries are contained in F. S. Regs., Part II, and the Staff Manual respectively. Title pages will be prepared in manuscript.

Hour, Date, Place.	Summary of Events and Information.	Remarks and references to Appendices.
Poona. 18.9.14.	Captain Dickson rejoined the Regiment, & was appointed O.C. Depot.	

Army Form C. 2118.

12

WAR DIARY
INTELLIGENCE SUMMARY.
(Erase heading not required.)

Instructions regarding War Diaries and Intelligence Summaries are contained in F. S. Regs., Part II, and the Staff Manual respectively. Title pages will be prepared in manuscript.

Hour, Date, Place.	Summary of Events and Information.	Remarks and references to Appendices.
Poona 21/9/14	150 shirts (warm) bought from 2nd Dorset Regt.	

Gulab Singh & Sons, Calcutta—No. 22 Army C.—5-8-14—1,07,000.

Army Form C. 2118.

WAR DIARY
or
INTELLIGENCE SUMMARY.

(Erase heading not required.)

Instructions regarding War Diaries and Intelligence Summaries are contained in F. S. Regs., Part II, and the Staff Manual respectively. Title pages will be prepared in manuscript.

Hour, Date, Place.	Summary of Events and Information.	Remarks and references to Appendices.
Poona 23.9.14.	Browning of Lance Heads &tutto commenced.	

Army Form C. 2118.

14

WAR DIARY

INTELLIGENCE SUMMARY.

(Erase heading not required.)

Hour, Date, Place.	Summary of Events and Information.	Remarks and references to Appendices.
Poona 28.9.14	Inoculation of the Regiment against Enteric commenced by troops.	

Army Form C. 2118.

15

WAR DIARY
INTELLIGENCE SUMMARY.
(Erase heading not required.)

Hour, Date, Place.	Summary of Events and Information.	Remarks and references to Appendices.
Poona 6.10.14	48 men attended a short course of instruction with the 82 batty. R.F.A. in disabling, serving & limbering guns. Lieut. E.W. Sprague returned from M.C. in England. Grp	

Army Form C. 2118.

16

WAR DIARY
or
INTELLIGENCE SUMMARY.

(Erase heading not required.)

Instructions regarding **War** Diaries and Intelligence Summaries are contained in F. S. Regs., Part II, and the Staff Manual respectively. Title pages will be prepared in manuscript.

Hour, Date, Place.	Summary of Events and Information.	Remarks and references to Appendices.
From 7.10.14	Borrowing of lance heads & butts completed	

Army Form C. 2118.

WAR DIARY
INTELLIGENCE SUMMARY.
(Erase heading not required.)

Instructions regarding War Diaries and Intelligence Summaries are contained in F. S. Regs., Part II, and the Staff Manual respectively. Title pages will be prepared in manuscript.

Hour, Date, Place.	Summary of Events and Information.	Remarks and references to Appendices.
Poona 8.10.14	Lt E.W. Spugin rejoined from M.C. in England.	

Army Form C. 2118.

18

WAR DIARY
INTELLIGENCE SUMMARY.
(Erase heading not required.)

Instructions regarding War Diaries and Intelligence Summaries are contained in F. S. Regs., Part II, and the Staff Manual respectively. Title pages will be prepared in manuscript.

Hour, Date, Place.	Summary of Events and Information.	Remarks and references to Appendices.
Poona 9.10.14.	Further instruction of same men with 82 battery R.F.A. Warm Serge clothing issued to 10guards —	

Army Form C. 2118.

19.

WAR DIARY
or
INTELLIGENCE SUMMARY.

(Erase heading not required.)

Instructions regarding War Diaries and Intelligence Summaries are contained in F. S. Regs., Part II, and the Staff Manual respectively. Title pages will be prepared in manuscript.

Hour, Date, Place.	Summary of Events and Information.	Remarks and references to Appendices.
Poona 10.10.14.	Warm Serge clothing issued to 1½ Squadron.	

Army Form C. 2118.

WAR DIARY
or
INTELLIGENCE SUMMARY.
(Erase heading not required.)

Instructions regarding War Diaries and Intelligence Summaries are contained in F. S. Regs., Part II, and the Staff Manual respectively. Title pages will be prepared in manuscript.

Hour, Date, Place.	Summary of Events and Information.	Remarks and references to Appendices.
Poona 12.10.14	Warm serge clothing issued for 1st Brigade. 24 Recruits passed Riding School Musketry. Authority Telegram No. 889/15 Orders received that 29th Lancers will take place of the 17th Cavalry in the Cavalry Division. Simla	

Army Form C. 2118.
21.

WAR DIARY
or
INTELLIGENCE SUMMARY.
(Erase heading not required.)

Instructions regarding War Diaries and Intelligence Summaries are contained in F. S. Regs., Part II, and the Staff Manual respectively. Title pages will be prepared in manuscript.

Hour, Date, Place.	Summary of Events and Information.	Remarks and references to Appendices.
15/08/14	Regiment received orders to entrain for Bombay	
Authority	⎧ 1 Train (1½ Squadrons) 1.59. a.m Wednesday 14th	
Telegram no 603 from AHQ Simla	⎨ 1 Train (1½ ") 1.34 a.m Wednesday 14th "	
	⎩ 1 Train (1 Squad + HQ) 1.59 Thursday 16th	
	Issue of warm clothing forwarded	
	The 1.59 Wednesday train was started from Poona Station three being put in one night.	
	The 1.34 Wednesday train from Kirkee Station baggage alone being put in one night.	

Army Form C. 2118.

22

WAR DIARY
or
INTELLIGENCE SUMMARY.
(Erase heading not required.)

Instructions regarding War Diaries and Intelligence Summaries are contained in F. S. Regs., Part II, and the Staff Manual respectively. Title pages will be prepared in manuscript.

Hour, Date, Place.	Summary of Events and Information.	Remarks and references to Appendices.
14/10/14. Authority Telegram no 603 from HQ Simla	C Squadron / MR. leave Ghorpuri Station 1.59 a.m. Thursday morning. Will be joined in due course with baggage	Telegram no 603. HQ Simla

Army Form.C. 2118.

23

WAR DIARY
or
INTELLIGENCE SUMMARY.

(Erase heading not required.)

Instructions regarding War Diaries and Intelligence Summaries are contained in F.S. Regs., Part II, and the Staff Manual respectively. Title pages will be prepared in manuscript.

Hour, Date, Place.	Summary of Events and Information.	Remarks and references to Appendices.
18/10/14 Bombay Docks S.S. Chyebassa Baroda	C Squadron HQ arrived Bombay 9.30 am proceeded on board the SS City of Baroda. A, B & D Squadrons camped out Wednesday night. Proceeded on board SS City of Baroda & SS Grogary. Open Thursday morning. At B Squadron & Grogary HQ & 2 Sec of D Squadron. C & D " + HQ & 2 Sec of B Squadron on SS Chyebassa. 2 Sec 30 men C Squadron on SS Baroda. SS Grogary left can at 11 am not of dock into midstream 5 pm 6.30 pm. SS City of Baroda	

Army Form C. 2118.

24

WAR DIARY
or
INTELLIGENCE SUMMARY.
(Erase heading not required.)

Hour, Date, Place.	Summary of Events and Information.	Remarks and references to Appendices.
16/10/14 Bombay Harbour	Ships lay off in Bombay harbour officers & men on shore. Returns for our muster drawn from units, men sorted. The harbour was lit by search lights.	

Instructions regarding War Diaries and Intelligence Summaries are contained in F. S. Regs., Part II, and the Staff Manual respectively. Title pages will be prepared in manuscript.

Army Form C. 2118.

25

WAR DIARY
or
INTELLIGENCE SUMMARY.
(Erase heading not required.)

Instructions regarding War Diaries and Intelligence Summaries are contained in F. S. Regs., Part II, and the Staff Manual respectively. Title pages will be prepared in manuscript.

Hour, Date, Place.	Summary of Events and Information.	Remarks and references to Appendices.
17/10/14 – 31/10/14 S.S. City of Baroda	The horses were exercised every mor. & eveg at night. They were fed at morg. & 5.30 p.m. 3 horses that were unfit when ship sailed it was changed to 6 & 10 hars & 10 oats. Also suffrs Sundo Sauro Rubs & everything were arranged for one to have. Since we joined 34th & 12 M Indian Sepoys so were sufficient M.A. Zgaff & Straggers and after they had four were next thought to a leg. Horses regulred, if you have any. We have them were away cases of fever or foals but on the have long length of deck in cut on the Temperant we went down a gale. Owing to breakage of the custom agrees were sunned in the hold. Used to the main equipment. Mules were started in the Pote. The Ammo & rifle were occupy but the top of the 1st of the Deck. And in the fore & aft shps it was expected but the top of the hold. It was really a quite custom brandt or hung say for further levato be only went & they gave on the. Recd by the R.S.A. Eny trops & commanders were every mingrno ludango ropecyl to Bullhum. Outpost the they in their town fort beyond of the gus. The run ran from mggk morngt twenty. He arrived of Sues on the eveg of 29th October & weighed Port Said sports on the mrng of 31st. B/d Port Said & Bds of 2 Offs wt B. Oy went with Gujerats to El Harttya on arr. from the shore	

War Diary
29th Lancers
From 1-11-14
To 29-11-14
Volume
pp 6

Army Form C. 2118.

WAR DIARY of 20th Cavalry
or
INTELLIGENCE SUMMARY

(Erase heading not required.)

Hour, Date, Place.	Summary of Events and Information.	Remarks and references to Appendices.
1st November 1914 to 6th November 1914. S.S. City of Benares	On board the City of Benares. We experienced very good weather. One horse died early on the 9th.	
7th – 9th November	Days on the 1st & went in shore. It was light preceded by disembark. The Regiment disembarked on 9th 11.30. The Squadron detrained & proceeded that night to the Camp South. A Squadron came up on Sunday morning but the other two drew up near MHQ. Regimenting reached in the ordinary. We HQ are at the City of Benares to be unloaded in Camp Sunday.	Left Base Headquarters Marseilles
10th – 11th November in Tier	N.S.H. He received orders to entrain as follows: "A" Squadron + HQ Monday night (9th Nov.) "C" " MG garden "B" + D Squadron Tuesday Morning (10th Nov.)	
12th – 14th November Camp La Source	We arrived at Orleans Thursday & were all encamped at La Source that night. We moved with us one Brigade of French Infantry. British Volunteers one left of Marseilles Signal indentary discontinued. We understand we are to form an advance army on the man at Marseilles. One horse died at Marseilles one other one trans. W. E. GREGORY 4 PEAR on transit	

WAR DIARY of 29th Lancers

from Nov 1st - Nov 30 - 1914

INTELLIGENCE SUMMARY.

Army Form C. 2118.

(Erase heading not required.)

Hour, Date, Place.	Summary of Events and Information.	Remarks and references to Appendices.
	One wing B Squadron was left in the depot at MARSEILLES. A/Major & Major J.T. HOLMES Remained in command of this at LA CROTTE and also for 22 hours the Depot S/charger & Major G. Smith the A/Major G. [?] Lt James I.A.L. joined the regiment on the 10th November. B/[?] of G.H. [?] was the machine Sund now knows at Orleans to replace one which had been given back to the Divisional sqn in exchange. This [?] Bramho occurred in regt. hqrs in Squadron the whole of which was organized — as in Squadron the men who had arrived [?] were organized in 1st line transport, transport [?], ten churchhorses, carts one hundred men. It is on file 12th 13th [?]. During the good work their man Three one cage of mules [?] had been sent to a Squadron sent, so that if in [?] be [?] 5 men alone seen. We received 17 horses from the Remount Depot Atla Crotte; having not which [?] 22. we [?] actually received [?] on, since in the whole campaign. the main troops were light & compact. our had with us hitherto the [?] [?] the 12 man of the [?] or entrenchment; [?] had with [?] the Orig.), they [?] explicit with sufficient hay [?] sorry in [?] [?] meals visit on the 22nd to Marseilles to have them cut. We have had no ([?]) W.E. Cent with 24 men of the 1st as enforcement	

Army Form C. 2118.

WAR DIARY of 29th Lancers
INTELLIGENCE SUMMARY. Month of Nov. 14
(Erase heading not required.)

Instructions regarding War Diaries and Intelligence Summaries are contained in F. S. Regs., Part II, and the Staff Manual respectively. Title pages will be prepared in manuscript.

Hour, Date, Place.	Summary of Events and Information.	Remarks and references to Appendices.
CAMP LA SOURCE ORLEANS. Nov.	We had also been ordered to join in of 15th Hussars of R.A.F. The men turned up on the 27th and [?] the men were left behind on the station on the 27th. The men in Serapheim [?] and have been ordered to go to sea. Left 19 when free of infection. He had a bad outbreak of horse on the right of Nov 21st/22nd 23rd. [?] more [?] horses. Some were caught after 24 hours we could [?] Known the next day we got them [?] the last one. The [?] report was to have 4th & 5th Sqn transport had [?] the [?] party in pattern on the 28th [?] these orders were cancelled as we had extra waggons on 2 out the Resdt [?] out [?] the intention [?] 4th at Marseilles was joined us about the 12th N. Bhadaur, Sadu Rissen Officers, was posted to the regiment on the 20th The road [?] Marseilles [?] amount [?] was a great deal of trouble as the cold. They had [?] [?] 53 men in a Serapheim [?]. On the 29th we have 23 men in hospital 33 men in a Serapheim camp. The 6 new casualties on the same date are 7 dead, 1 in Tent Hospital at Marseille, one in No 17 Hospital [?] Circlé The horse hair increased that is in [?] in the morning one on the [?] [?] a lot had casual expenses [?] Our ship [?] [?] these [?]	

WAR DIARY or INTELLIGENCE SUMMARY

Army Form C. 2118.

(Erase heading not required.)

Hour, Date, Place.	Summary of Events and Information.	Remarks and references to Appendices.
CAMP LA SOURCE. ORLEANS Nov.	No Regimental parade. Squadron drill was practised. On Wednesday the 25th the regiment went to LAERCOTTE range, where the new rifles were tested. The Machine Guns went on these occasions, the first time the guns had cut fire with, but the aim of fire all went well. Regimental rifle drill was practised when new practices in firing & unfixing bayonet — pointing & parrying with the Bayonet. Everyone drilled hard on him every movement & warn him rounds to get him accustomed to fort work — unless he both carry, are both have been well present. Hereby sweet changed all horses that stumbled have been kept equally one, & we have been given. The Regiment has proceeded to unhamper the Cheval when posted in the Churn. 18 Nov — But the aim was executed. 25 AT DRIVE? Two rifles fitted on Mumbras, & cannot shift, firing on an — the Companion of gun Machine Minerolius were also drawn for the regiment — the GOC the Brigade having found fault with the old "Re Smith & Westmire Staff" — one out of three Gr Stewards 29 Lancers Guns & Westmire Staff — the rest of the new Guns from the Ordnance	

The GOC the Brigade having found fault with the old "Re Smith & Westmire" command 29 Lancers Guns & Westmire Staff — the rest of the new Guns from the Ordnance

War Diary
of
9th Lancers
From 1-11-14.
To. 30-12-14

Volume I
Pp 6 - #32

121/4046

Army Form C. 2118.

WAR DIARY
or
INTELLIGENCE SUMMARY. From 1st - to 30th November

(Erase heading not required.)

Instructions regarding War Diaries and Intelligence Summaries are contained in F.S. Regs., Part II, and the Staff Manual respectively. Title pages will be prepared in manuscript.

Hour, Date, Place.	Summary of Events and Information.	Remarks and references to Appendices.
1st November 1914 to	On board the city of Benares. We experienced very rough weather	
1st November 15.14	on the head seas on the 2nd. We arrived at Marseilles about	
	2pm on the 3rd & went on shore that night. Proceeded to	
3rd to 6th November	Manoeuvre. J. Squadron came in at 10.30 7.am & another	
CAMP DORELY	Manoeuvre proceeded that night. M first Booth NSquader	
7th to 9th November	came up on Sunday morning. with the shared the going was all the	
	(Cap?) Squaden arrived in the afternoon. the refremely on the 8th on all the	
10th 11th November	night. the remained in camp [?] on Sunday following	
in train	A Squadron HQ Mator cyclists 9th Nov	
12th 14th November	& 1 Machine gun	Bee Headquarters
CAMP LA SOURCE	& 1 ½ Reinforcements	Marseilles
	B. D Squadron Quarter Master 10th Nov	
	& the rest of our [?] Brigade hospital + 1 spare all remained at	
	La Source that night. We proceeded with no Baggage to	× Motor
	First of machine guns & a Brigadier with regard of business the	× 1 geo.
	arrived acting transformation. We entrained him to & from an	
	outpost acting distribution. heights were begun in the rear of Marseilles	× Reinforcement

Gulab Singh & Sons, Calcutta—No. 22 Army C.—5-8-14—1,07,000.

Army Form C. 2118.

27

WAR DIARY
or
INTELLIGENCE SUMMARY.

From 1st - to 30th November

(Erase heading not required.)

Instructions regarding War Diaries and Intelligence Summaries are contained in F. S. Regs., Part II, and the Staff Manual respectively. Title pages will be prepared in manuscript.

Hour, Date, Place.	Summary of Events and Information.	Remarks and references to Appendices.
Camp La Source 15th November November	On the rose B Squadron was split in 7th Hospital at MARSEILLES, 45 Horses + 10 men of 1st: Holmes were sent to Remount Depot at LA CEROTTE, indent put in for 22 horses for N°s and 3rd chargers, Mr. Medical Officer (vet) + 1st A. vet captains Capt James M.S. joined the regiment on the 15 November in the place of Lt. Holmes. Two machine guns were drawn at Orleans to replace ones which were given in each camp. Three cases of mumps occurred in regiment. Two in C Squadron the 24th Risaldar was invalided on 2nd Squadron. The one who had slight mumps was sent to Our 2nd Lieut bought twenty fork, 10 draught mules, 5 carts were landed on to moor the 12th + 13th November. During the next week there were three more cases. 3 mumps + one cut 6 3 mumps, the scout of the Regimental Cypher as though of how to wheel 51 men each He received 17 mares from the Remount depot for Cercotte. He also indented + received a supply of horse regimental property the Regiment was kept + occupied with the work of the troops - our RFA in experimental + put in right after ten fire going into position + taking up in a Regiment up Horse Artillery on leaving the Horse Brigade. They were explained right after the cut work the use 2 or 3 of the guns in experiment	

WAR DIARY
or
INTELLIGENCE SUMMARY.

Army Form C. 2118.

From 1st to 30th November

(Erase heading not required.)

Hour, Date, Place.	Summary of Events and Information.	Remarks and references to Appendices.
CAMP LA SOURCE ORLEANS Nov 2	[handwritten entries largely illegible]	

WAR DIARY
or
INTELLIGENCE SUMMARY.

(Erase heading not required.)

Army Form C. 2118.

From 1st to 30th Nov

Hour, Date, Place.	Summary of Events and Information.	Remarks and references to Appendices.
CAMP LA SOURCE ORLEANS Nov	No regimental parades. Service dress was finished as ordered by the 20th ult. The Indian Sqns went to LACROTTE Range where rifles were tested. The Indian Sqns went on three marches. The Regt lost the guns that had been bought out of the Regimental funds for use with the except of one Maxim and 1 Regimental Colt. All horses that attempted hair by hand grafts me. as have been when taken from the Regiment. 4 Mar + 31 Indu (Cpt) Mjr Mcllwen ... Maxims were also shewn for the regiment.	

War Diary
29th Lancers
From 6-12-14
to 31.12.14
Volume
Rt 6

Army Form C. 2118.

No 3

Original

I/29th Lancers
North Riding 31/12/14

30

ADJUTANT GENERAL INDIA
-5 JAN 1915
BASE OFFICE

WAR DIARY
or
INTELLIGENCE SUMMARY.

(Erase heading not required.)

Instructions regarding War Diaries and Intelligence Summaries are contained in F. S. Regs., Part II, and the Staff Manual respectively. Title pages will be prepared in manuscript.

Hour, Date, Place.	Summary of Events and Information.	Remarks and references to Appendices.
6th Decr 1914	Computation taken over by Lt Col Saunders under orders B.O.C. Regt. Orders recd to entrain early Tuesday 8th morning; details to follow. From Rail Sec St D Sqr & headquarters 4.25. (8th J'honteaux 8.5. 2nd months A. Sqr Thiecher, June 8 4.55. B Sqr Jul. Vet Sec 10.15 Two horses allowed for entraining amph. Train 3 Part of [ ] Principally Regulating Station Hazebrouck but ran late. D.T Sqr detrained at Vitry and went on to billets at Haut Rieny distance about one mile afternoon & evening 1.9". A.TB Sqrs drn detrained at Bergette after	

Gulab Singh & Sons, Calcutta—No. 22 Army C.—5-8-14—1,07,000.

WAR DIARY
or
INTELLIGENCE SUMMARY.

Army Form C. 2118.

(Erase heading not required.)

Hour, Date, Place.	Summary of Events and Information.	Remarks and references to Appendices.
9th & 10th December	dark. A Squadron marched to Billets about 5 miles which were reached about midnight. Roads v[er]y	
15th	1 to 2 A.M. "B" Squadron went to 2. Billets were shaken & handed [to] Haut-Rieny next morning. At first only about 40% horses, all men under cover. Three men & six cook for Squadron. Route marching, trench digging & bomb throwing practised under Bongd arrangements. For day to day. Billetting are gradually enlarged. Steel Forters armoured command 10" Sqd via day. En: Cookers. English Horse shoes issued to replace Indian ones. Transport i.c. $59 G.S. Wagons, one Cook Cart & 4 horse G.S. Bags attached. One horse mean cook founded. 16th Prie with Lonner unfound.	

WAR DIARY
or
INTELLIGENCE SUMMARY.
(Erase heading not required.)

Army Form C. 2118.

Hour, Date, Place.	Summary of Events and Information	Remarks and references to Appendices.
22ⁿᵈ Sept.	On the night of 19th/20th a fire broke out at the farm of Mr de Haurd. Cause unknown. It was 9pm under control about mid night no damage done to horses or equipment. Total damage about £600-L Brigade.	
25th	Ordered to move to new billets, orders recv'd about 4.40 A.M. to move at once. Billets Occupied at St Hilaire about noon.	
	Whole Brigade ordered to move towards Heuchin about 5 miles. 29th Lancers Head quarters Nedon guns A.T.D. Sqs on aefers. Fontaines les Boulans B.T.C. Sqn Fiefs about 2 miles to east.	
30 31st Sept	Exercising — digging — route marching, foraging	

Lucknow

121/4401

WAR DIARY
OF
29th Lancers.
From 1st January 1915 TO 29th January 1915

Army Form C. 2118.

WAR DIARY
or
INTELLIGENCE SUMMARY.

(Erase heading not required.)

Army Form C. 2118.

ADJUTANT GENERAL INDIA
-7. FEB. 1915
BASE OFFICE

No 3 Section
A. G's Office at Base
I.E. Force
Passed to _____
S_____

Instructions regarding War Diaries and Intelligence Summaries are contained in F. S. Regs., Part II, and the Staff Manual respectively. Title pages will be prepared in manuscript.

Hour, Date, Place.	Summary of Events and Information	Remarks and references to Appendices.
1. 1. 15	Capt Hemans reported his departure to take Command of the Signal Squadron 2nd Ind. Cav. Div.	
4. 1. 15	35 men, 35 horses arrived as reinforcements from Marseilles.	
5. 1. 15	Leave given for four days — (Ind. of Poland, availability) Leave closed	
7. 1. 15.	Leave stopped. Regiment ordered into trenches for 48 hours from the evening of the 9th.	
8. 1. 15.	Asked available strength of rifles. Regiment could take into trenches — Reply 310 rifles besides 3 troops without their machine guns viz 20 men — Later received orders to proceed with 300 rifles, with 200 rounds per rifle and 2 machine guns with 3000 rounds each at noon 1/4th enough to 11 am) on proceeded to BETHUNE on 9th at noon (1/4th enough to 11 am) in trenches — Also Remt & Officer, 2 I.O's, and M.G Officer to spend the night in the trenches & acquaint themselves with the situation — night in the trenches & acquaint themselves with the	Weather up to 9th Jany wet — not very cold — began clearing up 9th.

WAR DIARY or INTELLIGENCE SUMMARY

Army Form C. 2118.

Hour, Date, Place.	Summary of Events and Information	Remarks and references to Appendices.
9 - 1 - 15	Brigade arrived at "bulbuls" or Fosse 7 Nord abt 2 Bns & CRE 2 Bns were at 12.20 pm and detrained at 12.40. There was much difficulty in clearing the hd Coys of bulbuls to make up the detachments at Floris. The Regiment arrived at Brigade rendezvous at 2 pm and at BETHUNE at 2.30 Sept. The Regiment had rather late orders, sent on the 15th, were found ready fallen up. The Regiment followed in rear of the Bedfordshire Regt and marched off in rear of the K.D.Gs, travelling through Beuvry and Annequin and — The Regt arrived at Rue de BETHUNE where the Brigade had been up its quarters to the action at 7.30 pm & looked about to move. A half Coy was made here abt 9 pm. But the leading regiments getting together and covering works with narrow roads. The move up of the Regt had been very between Beuvry and Hinges lane — At 9 pm the Regt moved off with Guides who were attached & had A and B Squadrons & their positions on the two trenches which they found had got about 3 & 4 pars of roads on them throughout the whole length — A and D Rd previously left there elements at the rear camp bulbuls — C Squadron had a guide sent to the supporting trench — Head Quarters and B Squadron also led by	
	Guides, went to the bulbuls & the .... (continues) The machine guns under Captain Martin .... Position previously .... The line the Esquadrons .... as taken now at 9.30 pm then H.Q. A B C Sqdns & victory when different 5. 24th Division left from here across	

WAR DIARY
or
INTELLIGENCE SUMMARY.

Army Form C. 2118.

(Erase heading not required.)

Instructions regarding War Diaries and Intelligence Summaries are contained in F. S. Regs., Part II, and the Staff Manual respectively. Title pages will be prepared in manuscript.

Hour, Date, Place.	Summary of Events and Information	Remarks and references to Appendices.
9-1-15	D Sqn. followed by the M.G. Section which came into position on the left of it, reached the left portion of the enemy lines and held it about an 5′5″ wounded in the nose near the entrance to the trench. When they were under a heavy and hot directed fire. The M.G. crew were rendered useless by the hvd. which fell into and onto it while taking up the position. The enemy line had been approached by a road, as the approaches trenches were full of water. A Sqn. followed D at an interval of about 15 hours and had Rathore and 7 is wounded at the same place as D had. The Cavalry had at all the Cavalry took place Major the Lighty 2 Havarney they have taken the line into strong a drop. Now water was left of their wounded themselves - after the line had been over-run, about 15 trying to disembark the night but the line was MG were ward last as the first Aid Post was established at Regtl H.Qrs. but was found too cramped and was moved near any before daylight to another building further N.	
+ about 11·30 p.m.	transported men began to arrive about 1 am. The stretcher bearing parties very inefficient - all cases were dressed by us and all but one were evacuated about 10 am have established horses to the Field Am. train once.	
10·1·15.	The remainder of the "D" Buffs Cheydrosh brought up at 1 am others came that the Bde. would keep up its attack when the 1st Bty. Division advanced and attack about 2 from South of the Canal. These orders	brought from clay night first aid

WAR DIARY
or
INTELLIGENCE SUMMARY.
(Erase heading not required.)

Army Form C. 2118.

Hour, Date, Place.	Summary of Events and Information	Remarks and references to Appendices.
10-1-15	Collected instructions to began the first trust at trenches at 2.55 am. Bring the telephone bring further. The message was sent by two orderlies following each other. Fire was kept up during the day and up to 5.15 pm. the fight was began. This was carried out with only one casualty and was Carrier Sec. Lee RAHMAN KHAN II shot in Shown. The night was passed quietly with the enemy about 15 firing. At 11 am orders were received to send a working party to relieve the double of supports trenches were always kept thin. General Communications — trenches were made to provide accommodation to the firing line —	Recommend Lt. O.P. for gallantry. L/Dfdr 2339 Dfdr Mjr ALI. R. 2335. Sec. Lee RAHMAN KHAN II
11-1-15	Above 3. Inverness a telephone message was sent to support trench as a firing line and preach in the entry telephone. The night branch was on Quetta and the supports trench was comparatively dry, and improvements during the day made it fairly comfortable, but however there was no place to get from it. Some 200 yards were quite impossible, he (illegible) on his line and. This trench was broken down up to 5 k Des. Very bad — It has had reached an arrival out to the 1st Coy. Casualty nil. Supply trenches were occupied by 6.30 am. About 10.15 am shelling the enemy's trenches & redouble fruits patrol (maintained shelling the enemy had without shelling the night — as they showed no activity — his activity of the Austrian returned after coming under fire and who had ... of the Afghans were hurried to trench line of trenches as previously. The rear enemy was hurried & trenches line of trenches as previously. The rear of the Afghans most afterwards except for one short burst of shrapnel from the enemy about 2 pm which fell just behind the Support trench Des.	Shown further Shown later

WAR DIARY
or
INTELLIGENCE SUMMARY.

(Erase heading not required.)

Army Form C. 2118.

Instructions regarding War Diaries and Intelligence Summaries are contained in F. S. Regs., Part II, and the Staff Manual respectively. Title pages will be prepared in manuscript.

Hour, Date, Place.	Summary of Events and Information	Remarks and references to Appendices.
	About 5:30 pm I heard the fire at 14 men previously reported missing coming slate in over original trench, having expended all their ammunition — asking for orders — I immediately wit over them — About 8 pm. to facilitate our ultimate withdrawal I gradually withdrew men from the firing line, supports & reserves, who were likely to impede the march some distance from nothing but a few that ale — Soon after 8 pm. I heard the 2 Leaders had left Rue de Bethune — ? but the C.O. the Regt. at the head the Return & was making supplement the Westmisters, and we effected the relief by 8.35 pm. one machine gun being left in position to cover the use of the relieving regt. — the 24th Lanciers moved off after collecting kits & so noting the casualties by 9.2 pm to Bethune, which we reached at 11.40 pm. — Entrenchment tools carried out after [crossed out] full the men had hadsome	× This sum was transfered a prominent point into now along which the enemy might advance.
12-1-15	Refreshment & Billets reached at 5-30 am Lr. Lt. Pollard rejoined from leave. 10.1.15. Left they well 7th L.H. together Lr. Knight proceeded on leave 12. v 13. with I. Reserve ammunition carried & pack mules held by Mounted men pending arrival (Limber waggons.	Bitter shining; not cold.

Army Form C. 2118.

WAR DIARY
or
INTELLIGENCE SUMMARY.
(Erase heading not required.)

Instructions regarding War Diaries and Intelligence Summaries are contained in F. S. Regs., Part II, and the Staff Manual respectively. Title pages will be prepared in manuscript.

Hour, Date, Place.	Summary of Events and Information	Remarks and references to Appendices.
15.1.15.	Actg R.M INDAR SINGH was murdered by Sow: 2305 SISRAM SINGH (JAT) who hurriedly committed suicide.	
22.1.15.	Casualties in actn 10.1.11 KIA's Duffr 2/1402 Arjun Singh. L/Dffr. 1855 Mamchund Singh. Wounded Nos: 1271. 2330. 2400. 2605. 2314. 1978. 2681. 2582. 2216. 2410. 1949. 1812. 2453. 2078. 2044. L. Shortridge temporarily attached to 17th Div. Ammunition (Gun-m) 4 Lancers 31 Lancers used in reinforcements Sowar No. 1512 Bhawan Sir 76 died of wounds rec'd. 10th.	Weather generally wet but frost set in on 27th Snow fell and thawed at on 31st. Second cold.
24.1.15 27.1.15		
29.1.15	26 Sowars from 14th Lancers received as reinforcements.	

A. R. Saunder L/Lt.
J. Rawen

Gulab Singh & Sons, Calcutta—No. 22 Army G—5-8-14—1,07,000.

Serial No 176

121/4719

WAR DIARY

29ᵗʰ Lancers.

From 2ⁿᵈ February 1915 to 8ᵗʰ February 1915.

Army Form C. 2118.

WAR DIARY
or
INTELLIGENCE SUMMARY. For February 1915

(Erase heading not required.)

Instructions regarding War Diaries and Intelligence Summaries are contained in F. S. Regs., Part II, and the Staff Manual respectively. Title pages will be prepared in manuscript.

Hour, Date, Place.	Summary of Events and Information	Remarks and references to Appendices.
2 Feb 1915	Regt. Orders 1st Indian Cav. Division 2 Feb. Part II. 2. The following promotions are made in the 29 Lancers with effect from the 15th Jan 1915 Ressaidar BADAN SINGH to Rissaldar vice Risseldar INDER SINGH deceased. Jemadar HAYAT ALI BEG to be Ressaider vice Resseidar BADAN SINGH promoted.	
8th Febr 1915	C. in C. awarded Indian Order of Merit 2nd Class to Jem: HAYAT ALI BEG for on the 11th January 1915 when orders to retire failed to reach him maintained with his party the defence of his batn of the trench through out the day, the remainder of the Brigade having withdrawn. A.R. Sanderson Lt Col 29 Lancers	Indian driver - no fact running to ?

WAR DIARY

29th Lancers.

From 15th February 1915 to 29th March 1915.

Army Form C. 2118.

29th Lancers.

WAR DIARY
or
INTELLIGENCE SUMMARY.

(Erase heading not required.)

Instructions regarding War Diaries and Intelligence Summaries are contained in F. S. Regs., Part II, and the Staff Manual respectively. Title pages will be prepared in manuscript.

ADJUTANT GENERAL INDIA
-7. APR 1915
BASE OFFICE

Hour, Date, Place.	Summary of Events and Information	Remarks and references to Appendices.
15. 2. 15	Jem: Bharat Singh (Jat) 16th Cav.y attached to regt. for duty.	
March 1st	Leave for officers stopped.	
2nd 3rd 4th	Working parties of 200 men provided by each regiment of Brigade on these days to dig line of trenches near St Venant, under supervision Sec. Field Engineers. Working hours 9 A.M. to 5 P.M. parties being taken to work trench daily by motor buses. Work mostly consisted of hurdle works.	Weather damp but very cold.
7th	Jem: Bhupur Singh and men of 2nd Lancers who accompanied required from India as 1st reinforcement been exchanged for men of 22nd Cav. (Roughers) under Jemadar Habib Khan	

WAR DIARY
or
INTELLIGENCE SUMMARY.

(Erase heading not required.)

Army Form C. 2118.

2 Lancers.

Hour, Date, Place.	Summary of Events and Information	Remarks and references to Appendices.
7th March.	Orders rec'd to change billets after dark and move to FONTAINES-LEZ-HERMANS. Marched 7 p.m. - occupied new billets by midnight. Distance about 5 m.	Weather hazard v7 cold. Some snow, wind.
8th, 9th, 10th.	Regiment under orders of immediate readiness. Heavy gun fire heard on 10th to Eastward.	
11th	Orders rec'd about 1 A.M. for Brigade to march at 4.30 A.M. By 8 A.M. the whole Brigade was hidden in BOIS DES DAMES - good cover among pines - rations carried up from road ¾ mile in evening - nights spent in bivouac. G	Warmer + dry. Drizzle and 12th.
12th	Capt. W. Z. BURMESTER 31st Lancers joined from M.H.O. Brigade. Orders rec'd to send a billeting party. Regt marched down to billets at AUCHEL, morning 13th. 13th Lancers relieved us.	
13th, 14th		Fair weather.

3
29th January

Army Form C. 2118.

WAR DIARY
or
INTELLIGENCE SUMMARY.

(Erase heading not required.)

Hour, Date, Place.	Summary of Events and Information	Remarks and references to Appendices.
15th March	Ordered to march midnight 14-15th to billets required to protect Flechin and Pippemont. Headquarters A & D Squadron to furnish B.C. & M.G.s to latter.	
17th	Moved from Flechin to La Tirmand. Pippemont detachment to Flechin.	
18th	Regt. Bde. Headquarters. 36th moved billets. Wild brigade reached post corps commander's to billet at Estrée Blanche with D Sqt at Flechinelle good billets.	
19th	Orders issued something is moved. All Indian ranks from detachment. Leaving in Europe. Alex. Penrice R.S.I. Com to heir & servant down allotted all from Flanders.	Some snow. Cold wind.
20th	Ch. Kendall the politic at D. 2 g Lancers known from the other corps. Lt. Colour appointed to the place. A. R. Saunders Lt. 2 Lancers	Winter weather. May 2nd 15th the reported today.

Serial No 176.

121/5504

WAR DIARY
OF
29's Lancers.

From 1st April 1915 To 30 April 1915

Army Form C. 2118.

WAR DIARY
or
INTELLIGENCE SUMMARY.

April 1915

Instructions regarding War Diaries and Intelligence Summaries are contained in F. S. Regs., Part II, and the Staff Manual respectively. Title pages will be prepared in manuscript.

(Erase heading not required.)

ADJUTANT GENERAL INDIA
-9. MAY 1915
BASE OFFICE

Hour, Date, Place.	Summary of Events and Information	Remarks and references to Appendices.
1.4.15 4	ESTREE BLANCHE. Companies 3, 4 & 5	Weather good to
2.4.15	Order to Brigade stand to from 4 pm until 6 pm when	but wind & fine day
	but delayed until next morning from the trenches	day Sun & Shy July
	Around L'ALLEU HONDEGHEM & L'AR & on breezer but Sun	
	Hour 6 pm to 8 East Side of which a front was	
	Ordered to hours St JEAN LEZ BISQUES. sent home round 5th to	
	reach Arberte Lys. Hours three Billets for approve	
	Major LAMBERT June 4. 4/4p.	
	2 L'AR MERCIE from March June 9/4/15	
	N.O. BADAN SINGH died wounds received in April	
	1/ BRADLEY gone for marching up R. KARAK SINGH	
15	16 men. 31 LANCERS 10.4.15	
	Cap MARCHANT Reg to Norfolks 9.4.15	
21.3.15?	D. of C DAYA SINGH from Hospital. Remounts up JAHAN SINGH sick in India	

Army Form C. 2118.

WAR DIARY
or
INTELLIGENCE SUMMARY.

(Erase heading not required.)

Hour, Date, Place.	Summary of Events and Information	Remarks and references to Appendices.

Instructions regarding War Diaries and Intelligence Summaries are contained in F. S. Regs., Part II, and the Staff Manual respectively. Title pages will be prepared in manuscript.

27.3.15 Dafdr Jagan Singh (31L) promoted Jem. vic Sawant Singh transferred to C.M.

1.4.15 Rec Ghulam Dastagir known from 19R vic Singh Badam died in the acting S.M.

17.4.15 Rec Chanda Singh promoted vic Harphul to C.M.
Lce Chattar Singh to duty vic Chanda Singh
Nabur Singh dead

17.4.15 Major B. Murray-White Gr Co Nicholson Lt Wedderburn obtain 8 Scottish sick furlough
Lt Cunningham Reid reported for duty from 1 month sick leave

28.4.15 [signature] Army Rera 1914

Serial No 146.

121/5799

WAR DIARY
OF
29th Lancers

From 1st May 1915 To 31st May 1915

WAR DIARY or INTELLIGENCE SUMMARY

Army Form C. 2118.

29 January [?] May 15

Hour, Date, Place.	Summary of Events and Information	Remarks and references to Appendices.
2. 15"	Marched with 1st Division on road. 6 A.M. to the Billets at HONDEGHEM. Major MURRAY WHITE sick to hospital	Cloudy hot air
4	Ordered 1st March back to old area	
5	Struck at 2:30 A.M. marched back 6 A.M. at Little B & C St at MAMETZ and A.D.H.Q. The squadron at CRECQUE four hours later	Weather fine & warm, lost to under relieve
9	1st Division to Left of 5 Sector. Ordered 2 hours notice from 5 A.M.	
12" 16 17	4 hours to readier 5 hours began 2 hours to stand to 10 A.M. 2 hours when prepare stand 10 A.M. Ordered to march to area w/ 127 on w/ Bryd. to be in Bethune Road Regiment in field Officers billets To Busleure Officers have billets A.D.H.S. have it open	Rain & weather is warm
18 19	Return 1st Std. billets my own & permanents CRECQUE 4 hours later	Slight change 13 & 19

Army Form C. 2118.

WAR DIARY
or
INTELLIGENCE SUMMARY.   May 1915.

(Erase heading not required.)

Hour, Date, Place.	Summary of Events and Information	Remarks and references to Appendices.
24	Jemadar Jawa Singh rejoined from hospital days ever [illegible]	Weather fine & warm
27	Representative to have to view HONDEGHEM West Lt [illegible] same will be before	
28	Regt with B Echelon ordered to move to [HAZEBR?] BRIDGE about 18 m to Houven t Ray to Field. 250 m [inclusive]. having orders to [illegible] at 1.15 p. Lt Col Parrere rejoined to-day 1 Brigr Show L/A Sounder Kingston Payne Burch Iryodes Arthur Hindson Matheson Jan [H?] Lds Sponge Munro Phili Shrubb [illegible] Kineter stay) with Corps. Radcd VIEUXBERQUIN about 6.30 p - regret to natural field & corn (with field. S Bradley ill A [cold]. [illegible] rain to form [illegible]	

Army Form C. 2118.

WAR DIARY
or
INTELLIGENCE SUMMARY.

3 29th Lancers May 1915

(Erase heading not required.)

Hour, Date, Place.	Summary of Events and Information	Remarks and references to Appendices.
30th	And Squadron savoured the trenches next to 1st front	Wilder villers etc
31.	1 Gd Dragoon Gds. relieved 2nd Royals Squadron of Regt went to trenches with S.I. on B Gurks Squadron for an hour returning 7.45 pm.	

A R Sanders Lt Col
29 Lancers

[STAMP: A.G.'s OFFICE AT THE BASE
21 JUN 1915
INDIAN SECTION]

Serial No 176.

121/6502

WAR DIARY
OF
29th Lancers.

FROM 1st June 1915 TO 30th June 1915

Army Form C. 2118.

29 Janr —

WAR DIARY
or
INTELLIGENCE SUMMARY.

(Erase heading not required.)

Instructions regarding War Diaries and Intelligence Summaries are contained in F. S. Regs., Part II, and the Staff Manual respectively. Title pages will be prepared in manuscript.

Hour, Date, Place.	Summary of Events and Information	Remarks and references to Appendices.

VLAMERTINGHE

Capt Mackie went out to join M. to order other Bns, they got (Capt's) in to shell the enemy. They were visited Maj Sinnes Kirkham for 2 R Irish end of 1.45 p. & then wanted a way out.

11 p.m. — Shrot orderly took 100 men as work party to assist sappers to dig CONNECTIVE TRENCH trench from Château 1 HOUSE (CHÂTEAU) to where there is no cover, but it had been shelled towards YPRES corner.

6 "   " took another 100 men to RLY DUGOUTS to the nails to them with 4 officers other orders to be ready to move up. Having [illegible] day as necessary

Again wired send help — Rd made to man the 1 p.m. 7.40 p.m. when I brought up to Rd between 6 & 30 Ch W own side of d. between VLAMERTINGHE & B rd &c.

Army Form C. 2118.

WAR DIARY
or
INTELLIGENCE SUMMARY.

30 November
(Erase heading not required.)

Hour, Date, Place.	Summary of Events and Information	Remarks and references to Appendices.
VLAMERTINGHE 3	accompanied by 6 others & 1 veteran machine guns or transport men. A little shooting + some rockets but it stopped and by 5-30 am. There was no more activity.	
4	YPRES canal, went to SALLY PORT. Only 1 prisoner of guard. took blankets back to lie upon and gave us about 10 min. Then marches via ECOLE to huts, YEOMANRY POST - lay down, the return to GHQ huts about 1.30 AM. Distributed rations, extremely tired, received Winchester met W/S ZILLEBEKE road. Started to arrive 2.15 & 4.15 AM. Then lay down to avoid being seen by Aeroplanes. Trench very shallow + no latrine accommodation. Half C Squadron 36' Machines to represent occupied trench — E of road. Trench only slightly shelled morning + evening. After dark improved trenches	Very hot day

Gulab Singh & Sons, Calcutta—No. 22 Army G—5-8-14—1,07,000.

Army Form C. 2118.

WAR DIARY
or
INTELLIGENCE SUMMARY.

(Erase heading not required.)

29 Squadron   June 15'

Hour, Date, Place.	Summary of Events and Information.	Remarks and references to Appendices.
YPRES	day between & communication trench to B6"	
	Return to bivouac after having received ordes	
	and 6 p.m. to return to old billets in built fields.	
	Carts arrived 9.30 p.m. loaded entirely with ammunition	
	sent them back under 2/Lieuts. Holmes	
	Welsh Cart was filled Evelling's returns came up	
5	in return of the 2 a/R	
	Regiment marched back via MENIN road 10.30 p.m.	
	getting in about 1. A.M. to sabullie	
	L/Cpl: Saunders took over Brigad Area to W/O/	
	Pollard who joined the dismounted party	
	Major Lambert reported to hospital (fever)	
	The enemy shelled the camp at about 8 p.m. and a few at	
7.16	9.30 pm Lieutenant hearn May Ullare was wounded —	
	Spahis Sheik 12 Cal Lillington some men & horses	

Army Form C. 2118.

WAR DIARY
or
INTELLIGENCE SUMMARY.

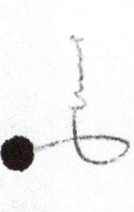

(Erase heading not required.)

Instructions regarding War Diaries and Intelligence Summaries are contained in F. S. Regs., Part II, and the Staff Manual respectively. Title pages will be prepared in manuscript.

Hour, Date, Place.	Summary of Events and Information.	Remarks and references to Appendices.
7.6.15. VLAMERTINGE	The Regt moved away from the camp on the brickfields to various fields round about.	
8.6.15.	Regt moved to Camp E "C" huts where the rest of the Bde were in huts.	
9.6.15.	Dug narrow deep trenches by the huts to occupy in case of being shelled	
12.6.15. 8.45 pm	Enemy shelled camp. Several shells falling within 300 yards of the huts	
13.6.15. 1 am	Huts again shelled. 4 shells falling amongst the trenches - no damage done to Regt - but in other brigades, 3 men were killed and 4 or 5 wounded. The shells were 100 prs.	
14.6.15. 7 am	Bde sent light in lorries 15 lb battery have arrived 9.00 am. Started for 14 Jansen [?]	
15.6.15.	Bde marched to MAMETZ [?] leaving at 8.15 am, and arriving	Weather for walk very hot for time in [?]
16.6.15. 6 am	at 1.25 pm about 22 miles. Rest at 4 hours in the Cass.	
30.30.C.	In billets until ordered to move	

28/6/15

A. R. Saunders Lt Col
2 R Sussex

Serial No. 196.

12/6502

WAR DIARY
OF
29th Lancers.

From 1st July 1915 To 31st July 1915.

Army Form C. 2118.

WAR DIARY
or
INTELLIGENCE SUMMARY.

29 Lancers July 1915

(Erase heading not required.)

Instructions regarding War Diaries and Intelligence Summaries are contained in F. S. Regs., Part II, and the Staff Manual respectively. Title pages will be prepared in manuscript.

Hour, Date, Place.	Summary of Events and Information.	Remarks and references to Appendices.
1st July	In billets - 4 hours water.	Weather generally fine. Met with some thunder storms.
6.	Parade mounted for Crown Prince of Servia.	
7.	Lt Cols: Pollard & L. Wingate ordered to report to War Office for orders. Reported departure.	Very windy S & S.W.
8.	A party of 250 men went to dig in 1st Army area. 2nd Rn & A.R. joined regmt Inspection of Corps by Lord Kitchener. Skeleton turn out. Digging party returned.	
11.		
15.	Lt Col: Saunders & Major Cheyne 8th (w): appointed 2/Lt: commandant & 2i/c command.	
17.		Weather during last half week very showery.
27.	150 men went to dig at Forêt in 1st Army area digging party returned.	

A. R. Saunders Lt. Col.
Comdg 29 Lancers

Serial No. 176.

12/6948

WAR DIARY
OF
29th Lancers.

FROM 1st August 1915 TO 31st August 1915

Army Form C. 2118.

WAR DIARY
29th Lancers
INTELLIGENCE SUMMARY
August 1915

(Erase heading not required.)

Hour, Date, Place.	Summary of Events and Information.	Remarks and references to Appendices.
31.7.15	Capt Marchant returned and Lt H D Ash Volunteer Officer joined regiment.	
1.8.15	Regiment marched SENLIS 13.M. Capt Burmester 2 Lt Shortidge left for marseilles. Major R.E. CHEYNE from 8th Cav joined regt as Second in Command.	
2.	Marched CONTRE 13.M. transport by roads about 16.M.	Slight rain.
3.	Marched FRANSU. 26 miles.	Heavy rain early morning slight during day.
4.	St LEGER 6 mls. few billets, horses out in fields.	
6.	Marched to FIEFFES (c. DSr.) MONTRELET 7 mls. billets poor very dirty. Capt HENDERSON vacated the field ambulance - frostbite in left arm.	Weather showery & chill.
11.	Lt SPURGIN vacated to field ambulance fever.	
20	2 Lt E.N.W JOHNSTONE I.A.R. joined regiment.	

Army Form C. 2118.

29th Lancers WAR DIARY or INTELLIGENCE SUMMARY.

(Erase heading not required.)

Instructions regarding War Diaries and Intelligence Summaries are contained in F. S. Regs., Part II, and the Staff Manual respectively. Title pages will be prepared in manuscript.

August.

Hour, Date, Place.		Summary of Events and Information.	Remarks and references to Appendices.
22	3 p.m.	Regiment started riding to FORCEVILLE Wood. about 18 miles. Travel party stayed night in wood. Lost horses under Major BIRCH returned to BEAUCOURT returned during day & got back to billets 11.30 p.m.	
23		During night 23-24 Lucknow Brigade Trench Party went to support at AUTHUILLE rest of Division occupied front line Section G1 - 2. near THIEPVAL	Weather fine till about 29th when storms began - it was raining to end of month.
		Regiment commanded by Major CHEYNE. Strength 8 B.O.s 10 I.O.s - 300 other ranks. Employed in putting village in state of defence + completing permanent trenches.	
31		One Squadron Bivouaced in GORDON CASTLE park; park unoccupied by CHEYNE LAMBERT BIRCH Capt MARCHANT MARTIN (Btn M.G Officer) TOWNSON. Lieut WRIGHT. BRADLEY. ASH 2/Lt RICE. JOHNSTONE. MERCER. Capt JAMES IMS	
30		L/F. FALCONER 2/L D.F CUNNINGHAM REID +R.L.N HERRICK	
		1 A.R. 2. 100 rank & file dismounted arrived from Base	
		L.E.W. SPURGIN rejoined from hospital	
		A. R. Sainm ? LM (a) 29 Lancers

Gulab Singh & Sons, Calcutta—No. 22 Army C.—5-8-14—1,07,000.

Army Form C. 2118.

WAR DIARY
of
INTELLIGENCE SUMMARY.
(Erase heading not required.)

Detachment 29th Lancers

Instructions regarding War Diaries and Intelligence Summaries are contained in F. S. Regs., Part II, and the Staff Manual respectively. Title pages will be prepared in manuscript.

Hour, Date, Place.	Summary of Events and Information.	Remarks and references to Appendices.
FIEFFES. 22.8.15. 3 pm	Detach[men]t of 300 rifles with remainder of Officers + extra men for led horses started	
MAILLY-MAILLET 11 pm	arrived + took post South of MAILLY-MAILLET.	
" 23.8.15. 12.45 am	Horses and lines billets started (relieve RAMM —	
" " 3 pm	M.G. Sections went into reserve Trenches at AUTHUILLE	
" " 7.45 pm	Detach[men]t started into trenches with 16 other French posts of the Bde.	
AUTHUILLE " 11.0 pm	arrived + took over duties of Reserve and garrison of AUTHUILLE	
" 24.8.15. 10 a.m.	B Sqn party (7 miles under Lt Ash) sent off in reserve 1-Subsector G 2	
" 25.8.15	working parties out	
" 26.8.15	do.	
" 27.8.15	do.	
" 28.8.15	do.	
" 29.8.15	do.	
" 30.8.15	do.	
" 31.8.15	do.	

R. R. Chenpr Major
Commdg Detacht

Serial No 176.

121/7286

WAR DIARY
OF
29th Lancers.

From 1st September 1915 TO 30th September 1915

Army Form C. 2118.

WAR DIARY
or
INTELLIGENCE SUMMARY.
Detacht. 9/29th Lancers
(Erase heading not required.)

Instructions regarding War Diaries and Intelligence Summaries are contained in F. S. Regs., Part II, and the Staff Manual respectively. Title pages will be prepared in manuscript.

Hour, Date, Place.		Summary of Events and Information.	Remarks and references to Appendices.
AUTHUILLE	1.9.15.	Working parties out	
	2.9.15	do - no-[word] D.B.Sgt. wounded	
	8.0 am	B.Sgt. party rejoined details	
	3.9.15 1.00 pm	Detacht. 34 Poona Horse relieved our detacht. which marched to Corbie FORCEVILLE and rested marts on on horses which retwrn	
FRECHENCOURT	6.30 am	arrived.	
MONTRELET	4.30 pm	Horse conducting party under S.D.O. to [?] rested White	
	8 pm	do -	
FRECHINCOURT	6.30 pm	Digging party of 300 men (including 100 Reinforcements just arrived from MARSEILLES) remained at FRECHINCOURT.	
SENLIS	4.9.15.	Two parties digging Trenches — from the FRECHINCOURT Dets.	
"	5.9.15	"	
"	6.9.15	"	(190 men returned to MONTRELET)
"	7.9.15.	One party of 131 men digging.	

Army Form C. 2118.

WAR DIARY
or
INTELLIGENCE SUMMARY.

2. Poona Horse   September

(Erase heading not required.)

Instructions regarding War Diaries and Intelligence Summaries are contained in F. S. Regs., Part II, and the Staff Manual respectively. Title pages will be prepared in manuscript.

Hour, Date, Place.	Summary of Events and Information.	Remarks and references to Appendices.
FRECHENCOURT 12.9.15	280 men + officers found digging parts at FRECHENCOURT through the night from MONTRELET	
13.9.15	MONTRELET, moved MARTINSART 7 p.m. relieved POONA HORSE in Reserve at AUTHUILLE at 3 a.m. under MAJOR LAMBERT and horse returned MONTRELET. under CAPT MARCHANT. (0 LANCERS in command Brigade. In reserve, digging parties morning + afternoon	
AUTHUILLE 13.9.15	Relieved 9th HODSONS HORSE (outposts) at 4 p.m. 1st RM KING C Squadron outpost (with Infantry) using relief & cover of 9th HH still - M.G. fire + heavy shelling from left flank - prepared laager at between 7 p.m - 9 p.m. met heavy shelling - 52 men hit + 2 wounded in B Squadron - during evening shell fell in hospital captured AUTHUILLE killing WAZIR SINGH - wounding NAND SINGH (Woronto Wald) + MULTAN (Lahore all) A Squadron	
14.9.15	Capt PIDDY (1st H.H. took patrol (2 men H.H. + Scouts) to point where prisoners had made a safe - they returned safely	

Army Form C. 2118.

WAR DIARY
or
INTELLIGENCE SUMMARY.

26 January ● ● September

(Erase heading not required.)

Instructions regarding War Diaries and Intelligence Summaries are contained in F. S. Regs., Part II, and the Staff Manual respectively. Title pages will be prepared in manuscript.

Hour, Date, Place.	Summary of Events and Information	Remarks and references to Appendices.
FRONT LINE TRENCHES G.I. Sector 15.9.15	5 men B Squadron wounded by sniper's grenade. Day very quiet. Bread ration of 6 grenades thrown between 7.10 pm. L/Spr Gein took out patrol towards point 405. Own Much Trench & machine gun fired from point 405.	Snowy, dull weather.
16.9.15	6 men wounded, 4 IASY, 2 IBSY. 2 Germans seen on parapet during day time – both were shot by our sniper. Relieved at 9 p.m. by 7 Gurkhas. Marched to FOREVILLE. Thence rode to FRECHENCOURT arriving 5 a.m.	
17.9.15	Rtd & B&L H MONRELET. FIEFFES arriving 10 p.m.	
20.9.15	Capt Rennick 11th Lancers arrived.	

Army Form C. 2118.

WAR DIARY
or
INTELLIGENCE SUMMARY.

29th Lucheux — 6th September

(Erase heading not required.)

Hour, Date, Place.	Summary of Events and Information.	Remarks and references to Appendices.
21st	Corps inspected by Lord KITCHENER.	
22nd 2 p.m.	Marched to new billets - head quarters A & C Sqs & M.G. at HARDINVAL - remainder at OCCOCHES about 1½ miles apart.	Weather changeable showery, dull.
24th 10 A.M.	Ordered to be ready for immediate move. Bedcloths + cook's kitchen - baskets with various rations for men under Brig-S. Transport Officer.	
26th	Two new Vickers Machine Guns received. One limbered wagon in want for the carriage. Issued M.G. section organised under 2 Lt. FALCONER. Limbered wagon for this taken from D Sq & replaced by G.S. wagon. Have hitherto countries complete with two requisite horses for M.G. & spare parts etc.	

A.Q. Saunders Major
O.C. 2/8 Lancers VMA

12/7601

Serial No. 176

Confidential

War Diary

of

29th Lancers

FROM 1st October 1915 TO 31st October 1915

343/A

In the Field
2-11-15

To

The Adjutant General
in India
Simla

Memorandum   War Diary of the
regiment for the month of
October 1915 is forwarded for
favour of disposal.

A. R. Sanders
Lt Col
Commanding 29th Lancers

Army Form C. 2118.

1 Div
29 Lancers
October
29 Lancers

WAR DIARY
or
INTELLIGENCE-SUMMARY.
(Erase heading not required.)

Instructions regarding War Diaries and Intelligence Summaries are contained in F. S. Regs., Part II, and the Staff Manual respectively. Title pages will be prepared in manuscript.

ARMY HEAD QUARTERS INDIA
C.F.L.
24 NOV 1915

Hour, Date, Place.	Summary of Events and Information.	Remarks and references to Appendices.
1 to 8"	HARDINVAL & OCCOCHES.	
9"	Moved billets to BOISBERGUES. Reorganised M.G. A.C. & D. Sqn & AUTHIEUX. B.Sqn about 2 m. less. Horses in open - cover for men available but not used.	1st - 31st Fine bright weather slight frost.
12"	Capt. RENNICK reported departure on transfer to 9 H.H.	
22"	Brigade moved to E.S. Rept. to billets PICQUINY 3 Sqn H.Q.rs 1 M.G. + St PIERRE A.GOUT. B Sqn later 2 men rec'd from monton to Le GARD. All horses remain under cover. Following promotions made. Q.M.r DUFF ABDUR RAHIM KHAN Kh. Tevaider Sqt 15th May Ressaldar GHULAM DASTAGIR KHAN to Risseldar Major Sgt 23rd Aug. Ressaider KABUL SINGH to Risseldar. Jemadar BHARAT SINGH to be Ressaidar. K.D. KHUB RAM to be Jemadar.	Weather generally fine throughout. Wind W. & S and heavy this is not enough + rainy towards end of month
24"	Ressaidar BHARAT SINGH ordered to rejoin his regiment 16th C. in PERSIAN GULF 7 left his duty. Lt. J. F. JOLLIT I.A.R. reported + arrived for duty.	
31"		

A. R. Saunders Lt. Col.
Cmdg 29 Lancers

Army Form C. 2118.

29th Lancers WAR DIARY October 1915
or INTELLIGENCE SUMMARY.
(Erase heading not required.)

Instructions regarding War Diaries and Intelligence Summaries are contained in F. S. Regs., Part II, and the Staff Manual respectively. Title pages will be prepared in manuscript.

Hour, Date, Place.	Summary of Events and Information.	Remarks and references to Appendices.
1st 8	HARDIVAL & OCCOCHES.	1st–31st
9"	Move billets to BOISBERGUES H₂dqrs HQ. A.C.D Sqn & AUTHIEUX	Fine bright weather slight frost.
	B Sqn about 2 miles. Horses in open - cover for men obtainable but not reqd.	
12	Capt RENNICK reported departure on transfer to 9th H.H.	
22	Bregde moved to S. Rgts to billets PICQUINY 3 Sk HQrs	Weather very dull fine throughout
	7 M.G. & St PIERRE A GOUY B Sqn Latters 2 men ridden & dismtd remainder marching to Le GARD. All horses & men under cover.	would but some heavy
	Following promotions made.	hits in early mornings
	Q Mr Duffr ABDUR RAHIM KHAN to be Jemadar 31-15th May	& rainy towards end of
	Rmdar GHULAM DASTAGIR KHAN to be Risseldar Major 31-23rd Aug:	the month.
	Remdar KABUL SINGH to be Rissaldar "	
	Jemadar BHARAT SINGH to be Ressaidar "	
	K. D. KHUB RAM to be Jemadar "	
24	Ressaidar BHARAT SINGH ordered to rejoin his regiment 11b (a)	
31st	& PERSIAN GULF & left this day.	
	2nd Lt. J.F. JOLLIT I.A.R. reported & arrived for duty.	

A. R. Saunders Lt. Col
Cmn 29 Lancers

Serial No. 176.

4480/E1

Confidential

War Diary

of

29th Lancers.

FROM 1st November 1915 TO 30th November 1915

S-75/A 2.12.15

The Adjutant General
India
Simla

Herewith War Diary of the regiment under my command for the month of November 1915 for favour of disposal.

A.R. [Sale?]
Lt Col
Commanding 29th Lancers

Delhi
29/12

Army Form C. 2118.

WAR DIARY
or
INTELLIGENCE SUMMARY.
(Erase heading not required.)

29th Lancers

November 1915.

1 DIV Rueck Bde

Hour, Date, Place.	Summary of Events and Information.	Remarks and references to Appendices.
1st to 19th Novr.	Regiment in billets. C.A.D.M.Gun at PICQUIGNY	
18th Novr	Regt changed billets. B sqdn at ST PIERRE A GOUY A.C.D.M.G. at CONDE FOLIE	
21st Novr	B and C sqdns moved to B sqdn at ETOILE. C sqdn to BETTENCOURT.	
4/15	Capt Z.G. Burmester 31st Lancers rejoined from Base	
7/15	2/Lt F.W. Herrick I.A.R. was attached to I.C.C. sqdn	
13/15	Reinforcement of 13 men joined	
23/15	Reinforcement of 7 men joined.	
16/15	Capt G. Marchant was attached to 1st Cheshires for a months training.	
16/15	2/Lt T.F. Falconer evacuated to hospital	
23/15	Capt M.W. Ogilvy evacuated to hospital	
25/15	Capt C.G. Henderson rejoined from England	
27/15	Capt C.V. Martin went as instructor to Machine Gun school.	
2"	To Sikh Rsm 14 Lancers (attached) promoted Ressaldar K. Bfr Tairaram from 14th Jemadar. Both entry from 24/10/15. A.R. Seymour Lt Col. Comdt 29th Lancers

Gulab Singh & Sons, Calcutta—No. 22 Army C.—5-8-14—1,07,000.

Serial No. 176.
121/7780.

CONFIDENTIAL

WAR DIARY

OF

29th Lancers

FROM 1st November 1915 TO 30th November 1915

Date	Summary of Events and Information	Remarks and References to Appendices
1st to 19th November	Regiment in billets. C.A.D. M.Guns at Picquigny B. Sqdn. at St. Pierre A Gouy.	
18th November	Regiment changed billets. A.C.D.M.G. at Conde Folie	
21st November	B and C Sqdns. moved to (B. Sqdn. at Etoile (Bettencourt	

Army Form C. 2118.

29 Lancers **WAR DIARY** or **INTELLIGENCE SUMMARY.**
(Erase heading not required.)

November 1915.

Instructions regarding War Diaries and Intelligence Summaries are contained in F. S. Regs., Part II, and the Staff Manual respectively. Title pages will be prepared in manuscript.

Hour, Date, Place.	Summary of Events and Information.	Remarks and references to Appendices.
15 to 19 Nov.	Regiment in billets. C.F.D.M.Gunt at PIQUIGNY B Sqdn at ST PIERRE A GOUY.	
18th Nov	Regt changed billets	
21st Nov	B and C Sqdns moved to BETTENCOURT *A.C.D.M.G. at CONDE FOLIE	
4/15	Capt L.G. Burmester 1st Lancers rejoined from Base	
7/15	2/Lt R.W. Herrick 1.7.R. was attached to 1.C.C. Sqdn.	
13/15	Reinforcement of 13 men joined.	
23/15	Reinforcement of 7 men joined.	
16/15	Capt G. Marchant was attached to 1st Cheshires for a month's training.	
16/15	2/Lt T.P. Falconer invalided to hospital	
23/15	Capt W.W. Ogilvy evacuated to hospital	
25/15	Capt C.G. Henderson rejoined from England.	
27/15	Capt C.V. Martin went as instructor to Machine Gun school.	
2'	Jr. Sahib Ram 14 Lancers (attached) promoted Risaldar. K. Dfr Tara Ram promoted Jemadar "Venedar" (acting) fr.24/11/15.	

Serial No. 176.

Confidential

War Diary

of

29th Lancers.

FROM 1st December 1915 TO 31st December 1915

T. 17/A 2.1.16

The Adjutant General
in India
Simla

Memorandum

Herewith War Diary of the regiment under my command for the month of December 1915 for favour of disposal.

C.R. Smith
Commanding 29th Lancers Lt Col

Delhi
26/1

Lucknow CAV Bde. 1 Ind Cav Div

WAR DIARY

29th Lancers

December 1915

Army Form C. 2118.

Instructions regarding War Diaries and Intelligence Summaries are contained in F. S. Regs., Part II, and the Staff Manual respectively. Title pages will be prepared in manuscript.

or

INTELLIGENCE SUMMARY.

(Erase heading not required.)

Hour, Date, Place.	Summary of Events and Information.	Remarks and references to Appendices.
1st 915	Hd Qtrs A,D Sqs & M.G. at CONDE FOLIE.	
8th	B. C. Sqn at BETTENCOURT. 2/Lieut J F FALCONER rejoined from hospital.	
16 & 31st	A, B, D Sqs and Hd Qrs L. SAIGNEVILLE	
	C Sqn L CAHON	
	M.G. L GOUY.	
14th	Capt MARCHANT rejoined after attachment to infantry for one month.	

A.R. Sanders Mjr.
Comdg 29 Lancers

29 Lancers Frukhmal Bde
1st 3rd Cav Bde

Army Form C. 2118.

WAR DIARY
INTELLIGENCE SUMMARY.
(Erase heading not required.)

JANUARY

Hour, Date, Place.	Summary of Events and Information.	Remarks and references to Appendices.
January 31.1.16	No change in billets, with exception of M.Guns who moved to Le Montant to be brigaded with the sections of 36th, JH & KKG's to form a M.Gun Squadron.	Weather generally milder with wet - cold weather with rain & snow frost
22nd	2/Lt T.Falconer reported from sick leave.	
26th	Capt C.O.E. Nicholson ordered to England.	
	During the month 10 men went to hospital 15 — arrived from here 7 — returned from hospital	

A.R. Selby Lt Col
cmdg 29th Lancers

192/A

On His Majesty's Service.

To The Adjutant General
in India

Simla

Zorawar Singh
29/L

1 DIV Cav Bde

115

WAR DIARY
-or-
INTELLIGENCE SUMMARY.
(Erase heading not required.)

Army Form C. 2118.

February 1916

29th Lancers

Hour, Date, Place.	Summary of Events and Information.	Remarks and references to Appendices.
5/2/16	No change in billets.	
	2/Lt CLARKE. L.C. ⎫ Special Reserve joined for duty with the Regt.	
	2/Lt FITZGIBBON. J.C.⎭ of officers	
7/2/16	2/Lt JOHNSTON. E.N.W. I.A.R reported sick	Walton grumbly for last six weeks. Invalid the end of the month with Enanit.
26/2/16	Major MARCHANT. G. appointed Instructor 1st Army School in the field	
	This officer was promoted to Major on 22.2.16 vide Gazette of India No 58. dt 21.1.16	
	2/Lt CLARKE *L.C. reported sick & evacuated to hospital	
	The M.G. section, consisting of 4 guns under 2/Lt A.A. MERCER and 2/Lt J. FALCONER was transferred during the month to form a portion of the Bde Machine Gun Sqdn.	
	During the month 10 men went to hospital	
	3 — joined from Base	
	4 — joined from Hospital	A.R. Sandford Lt-Col 29 Lancers

578/A 2-4-16

The Adjutant General
 Simla

Memorandum

Herewith War Diary for the month of March 1916 for favour of disposal.

M

R E Cheyne Lt Col
Commanding 29th Lancers

WAR DIARY

Army Form C. 2118.
(48)

1 Div Rural Bell
2.9 Lancers
March 1916

Instructions regarding War Diaries and Intelligence Summaries are contained in F. S. Regs., Part II, and the Staff Manual respectively. Title pages will be prepared in manuscript.

INTELLIGENCE SUMMARY.
(Erase heading not required.)

Hour, Date, Place.	Summary of Events and Information.	Remarks and references to Appendices.
26th	From 1st to 25th No change of billets since last month. 1st 2nd Cav. Divn, being now attached to the 3rd Army's area, the Regiment being billeted as follows:— HQ. A & C Sqdns at FONTAINE L'ETALON B Sqn ———————— CHERIEUVRE These villages occupied previously by French Cavalry were in an unsanitary condition and had also had sickness in them. All animals were ordered to be in the open; but later orders were received to disinfect all trans, stables etc. Admitted to hosp during the month 26 2 OR Rtd to Duties 3 Rejoined from Hosp 8 Jd from Base 20 P/Grrasaw M/Cpl Cmdg. 2.9th Lancers	Snow storm 21st – 26th made any being postponed on day one account of state of ground. Weather very fine from 27th onwards

Army Form C. 398.

To:— The A.G. in India.
Simla

DESPATCH.	RECEIPT.
Sender's No. 575/A	Date_____ hour_____ m.
Date_____ hour_____ m.	Signature:—
URGENT or ORDINARY.	

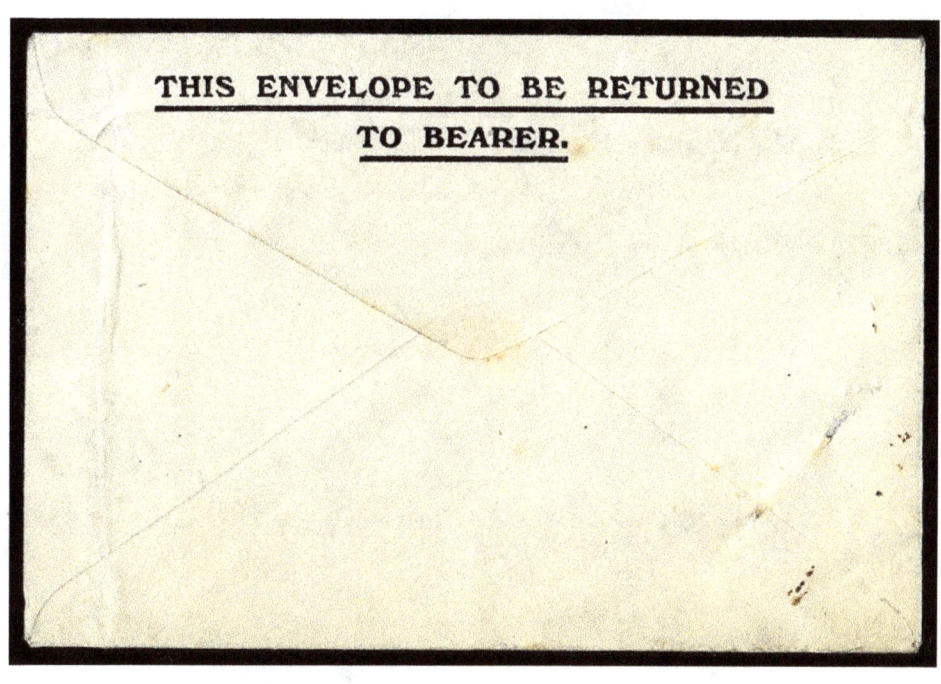

144/A   3-5-16

Confidential

The A.G. in India
                Simla

Memorandum

Herewith War Diary of the regiment under my command for the month of April 1916 for favour of disposal.

A. R. ——
Lt Col
Commanding 29th Lancers

M

Army Form C. 2118.

WAR DIARY

1 Div
29th Lancers (10)
April 1916

INTELLIGENCE SUMMARY.

(Erase heading not required.)

Instructions regarding War Diaries and Intelligence Summaries are contained in F. S. Regs., Part II, and the Staff Manual respectively. Title pages will be prepared in manuscript.

Hour, Date, Place.	Summary of Events and Information	Remarks and references to Appendices.
1st to 8th	A & C sqdns at FONTAINE L'ETALON & HQ Gro.	
	B & D at CHERIENNE	
9th to 14th	Regt. went out to Brigade training C & HQ Gro at VYRENCH A.B.D at VYRENCHEUX.	
15th	Regt. returned to Fontaine L'Etalon & Cherienne	
8th	2/Lt JOHNSTON I.A.R rejoined from hospital	
11 9/16	2/Lt FITZGIBBIN. Spec. Res. Offr. transferred to 13th Hussars.	
17th	Capt HENDERSON, I.P.O, 19 S.O.R to MARSEILLES for duty	
13th	Col CHEYNE attd. to 5th Corps D.irnl Cav School for month	
19th	Lt. B. BOGGS joined Regt in field from MARSEILLES	
	Capt G. W. HENNANS 1.9.13) granted temporary rank of major (without pay) Capt C. G. HENDERSON 2.1.16) Lt R.A. WIGHT 1.9.13) temporary rank of Capt (with ordy pay) Lt E. W. SPURGIN 1.9.13) Reinforcements from 45- Base during month 20 - O. R. S.	Casualty list with form shewing horse strens. Rept from Capt S went 6 hospt — Q.R.S. N Col Cmdg 29th Lancers

Gulab Singh & Sons, Calcutta—No. 22 Army C—5-8-44—L-07,000.

SERIAL NO. 176.

Confidential
War Diary

of

29th Lancers.

FROM 1st May 1916 TO 31st May 1916.

WAR DIARY
or
INTELLIGENCE SUMMARY.

(Erase heading not required.)

Army Form C. 2118.

29th Lancers

May 1916.

Hour, Date, Place.	Summary of Events and Information	Remarks and references to Appendices.
9.5.16.	Changed billets :- At first whole Regiment at CARETTEMONT.	
24.5.'16	A & C Sqdns moved to ETREE WAMIN.	
2/5/16	LT A.G. BOGGS reported sick	
11/5/16	2/LT V.A. HERBERT 2.A.R. joined	
15/5/16	LT COL R.E.CHEVNIX. returned from duty with 6th Corps.	
18/5/16	2/LT L.C. CLARKE Special Reserve of Cavalry joined from hospital	
19/5/16	2/LT J.C.T. O'CONNOR 2AR joined.	
11/5/16	The establishment of J.O.s increased to 23 (incl hos)	Lestin Qu'only ico seen
	NCOs —— 84 (" ")	
	The following J.O.s were promoted from that date	
	To be Ressaidars Jem. JAFFS.113 KHAN 22nd Cav.	
	Jem. BIHALAN SINGH	
	The following NCOs were promoted Jem. acting	
	2446. K.Nk. GULAB SINGH (B.)	
	2392 K.Dr. SIRI RAM (A)	
	1640 KOT THAN SINGH (B)	
	1313 Dr. IBRAHIM KHAN (C)	
	1471 Nk. JAG SINGH (A)	
	2227 Nk. NATHA SINGH (A)	
	Men evacuated sick 14 Reinforcements from Base 18 J.O.R.	
	Men rejoined from hosp 10	

C.R. Sa— *Lt Col*
Cmdg 29th Lancers

591/R   1.7.16

To   The Chief of General Staff
                  Simla

Memo:-
        Herewith War Diary of the regiment under my command for the month of June 1916 for favour of disposal.

           ARS———   Lt Col
       Commanding 29th Lancers

Book 13/4
1 DIV
Army Form C. 2118.

WAR DIARY
or
INTELLIGENCE SUMMARY.

29th Lancers.

June 1916.

(Erase heading not required.)

Hour, Date, Place.	Summary of Events and Information	Remarks and references to Appendices.
18/6/16	A working party of 6 BOs. & 300 Indian ranks under Lt Hotchkiss guns were sent up & help in carrying stores, trenching etc in the front line trenches. Major BIRCH Commanded. No: 2351 L/Dfr BAKHTAWAR SINGH (21D) } were killed by No: 856 Sr. NAND SINGH (31&D) } trench mortar (buried at AUBIN ST AUBIN) No: 681 Sr. SOWANT SINGH (31st &HO) } were wounded by No: 2897 Sr. URGEN SINGH } bombs. Party returned on 27/6/16.	Buried at not Aubin
25/6/16	Woordi Major Mahmed Umer Khan was murdered by Sr JAS RAM.	
30/6/16	Changed billets to MILLY.	
18/46	Iean THAN SINGH transferred to M.G. 5gn.	
	Rejd from Hospital 17 IORs Rein Jemnuta from Aume 35 IORs Sent to manships 2 IORs 20 men then evacuated (Hopl) 16 a R.S.A. Esal under 29th Lancers	

Gulab Singh & Sons, Calcutta—No. 22 Army C.—5-8-14—1,07,000.

Army Form C. 2118.

WAR DIARY
or
INTELLIGENCE SUMMARY.
(Erase heading not required.)

July 1916.

29th Lancers.

Instructions regarding War Diaries and Intelligence Summaries are contained in F.S. Regs., Part II, and the Staff Manual respectively. Title pages will be prepared in manuscript.

Hour, Date, Place.	Summary of Events and Information	Remarks and references to Appendices.
1st July	In billets at MILLY. at 2 hours notice.	
2nd July (-18th) 19th July	moved to VILLERS HOPITAL moved to CAMBLIGNEUL A working party of 7 B.O's & 300 Indian Ranks under Lt Col. RE CHEYNE went up to AUX RIETZ (part of the LABYRINTH) and worked in the trenches by NEUVILLE ST VAAST. from 20.7.16. to 31.7.16.	Weather mostly good in middle of the month. Remainder fairly heavy summer weather. All kinds of fruit in Season.
28 7/16	Jem. ARSLAN KHAN 27th L.O. Jem. BARLU SINGH 14th L. Jem. SULEMAN KHAN 39th C.I.H. & 47 J.O.R. joined from MARSEILLES in exchange to 1 party of 50 sent to go shortly (Aug 1st).	
8 7/16	MAJOR C.H. HENDERSON rejoined from MARSEILLES. During this month 12 men (G.O.R) went to hospital. 6 rejd from — 8 came up from turn.	

CR[signature]
Cmndg 29th Lancers.

Army Form C. 2118.

WAR DIARY
29 Lancers
INTELLIGENCE SUMMARY.
(Erase heading not required.)

AUGUST 1916.

126/A

Instructions regarding War Diaries and Intelligence Summaries are contained in F. S. Regs., Part II, and the Staff Manual respectively. Title pages will be prepared in manuscript.

Hour, Date, Place.	Summary of Events and Information	Remarks and references to Appendices.
1 8/16 CHELERS	Regt changed billets into training area as follows :—	
	H.Q, C & D sqdns to CHELERS	
	B sqdn to LE TIRLET	
	A — to HERLIN - LE - VERT.	
7 8/16	LT COL A. R. SAUNDERS left for a special appointment at MARSEILLES.	
	LT COL R. E. CHEYNE left to assume tempy cmd of 18th DURHAM L. Infantry.	
	Major P. B. SANGSTER D.S.O assumed tempy cmd of (2nd Lancers) the Regt.	GHQ 79 A/1538G.d.1.8.16
9 8/16 MARLINCOURT -LE-PAS.	Regt changed billets to MARLINCOURT-LE-PAS.	
10 8/16	A working party under MAJ HENDERSON comprised as follows	
	7 B.Os. 7 I.O.R. 8 J.O.s. 369 I.O.R. & 4 cooks marched to SOUASTRE, & being billeted there, worked nightly in front line by FONQUEVILLERS.	
11 8/16	2820 Sr. MAMRAJ (D sqdn) slightly wounded working party against Regiment.	
14 8/16	A patrol from A sqdn under LT RICE comprised of Jem NATHA SINGH	
15 8/16	2 NCOs & 5 Sowars left for BIENVILLERS for reconnaissance work in MARLUZEL.	
21 8/16	Regt moved into new billets at MARLUZEL.	
20 8/16	A sqdn patrol returned. Casualties nil.	

Army Form C. 2118.

WAR DIARY
INTELLIGENCE SUMMARY.

29th Lancers.

August 1916.

(Erase heading not required.)

Instructions regarding War Diaries and Intelligence Summaries are contained in F. S. Regs., Part II, and the Staff Manual respectively. Title pages will be prepared in manuscript.

Hour, Date, Place.	Summary of Events and Information	Remarks and references to Appendices.
WARLUZEL 29.8.16	A working party compred remdrs went up to relieve 36th 7H condn party. at BIENVILLERS. Major H. MEYNELL (D) Capt SPURGIN (C) Lt MORRITT (B) 2/Lt CLARKE (A) 4 IOS. 3 B.S.R. & 4 Corpls. 150 I.O.R. 2 cyclists	
30.8.16	Regt provided a hurdle-making party consisting of 125 I.O.R. 2 B.O.s; 2 I.O. at LUCHEUX work Hours 9 am - 4.30 pm daily, returning to Regt billets afterwards. During the month:— 13 men went to Hospital. 3 men retd from Hospital. 17 reinforcements came from MARSEILLES. 1 sweepers	

H. K. Birch. Major
Comdg 29th Lancers.

29th Lancers.

WAR DIARY
INTELLIGENCE SUMMARY. September 1916

Army Form C. 2118.

Hour, Date, Place.		Summary of Events and Information	Remarks and references to Appendices.
WARLUZEL	September 1st	2 men (Jats) to hospital.	Dismtd men were collected Divisionally & rejoined Regt on 1.x.16.
"	2nd	Trench working party returned. 1 I.O.R. (Cgdn) very slightly wounded.	
"	3rd	Regt marched to OUTREBOIS. (billets)	
OUTREBOIS	4th	2 men (1 Jat, 1 Mahn) to hospital.	During most of this period They were employed in making The Cavalry tracks up to LEUZE and DELVILLE woods.
		Regt marched to DOMVAST. (billets).	
		2 men (Jats) rejoined from hospital	
		2 men (1 Jat, 1 Mahn) to hospital.	
DOMVAST	5th–10th	Training (Divisional) in special training area.	
"	5th	1 Jat to hospl.	
"	7th	2 Jats from hospl rejoined.	
"	9th	1 Sikh to hospl	
"	10th	2 Jats to hospl	
		1 Jat rejoined from hospl.	
	11th	Regt marched to BEALCOURT (billets).	
BEALCOURT	12th	Regt marched to MILLY and BOUT DE PRES.	
MILLY	13th	Regt marched to QUERRIEUX (bivouac) [Divn concentrated]	
		1 Jat rejoined from hospital.	
QUERRIEUX	14th	MAJOR G. MARCHANT rejoined from Staff appt. (Army School)	
		7 I.O.R. (Jats) joined from Base.	

29th LANCERS.

Army Form C. 2118.

WAR DIARY or INTELLIGENCE SUMMARY.

September 1916 (continued)

Instructions regarding War Diaries and Intelligence Summaries are contained in F.S. Regs., Part II, and the Staff Manual respectively. Title pages will be prepared in manuscript.

(Erase heading not required.)

Hour, Date, Place.		Summary of Events and Information	Remarks and references to Appendices.
QUERRIEUX.	September 16th	Regt marched to DERNANCOURT (bivouac) arriving 10.15 A.M. (10½ miles). 2 Sikhs with dismtd men wounded.	at 5.10 am
DERNANCOURT.	" 16th	1 Sikh to hospital.	
	" 16th-25th	Patrols of 8 OR and NCOs sent up daily to LEUZE and DELVILLE Woods to reconnoitre route up.	
	" 16th	2 9OR (1 Jat, 1 Mhdn) rejoined from hospl.	
	" 19th	1 Sikh to hospital	
	" 21st	1 Sikh and 6 Jats joined from Base.	
	" 23rd	1 Jat to hospital	
	" 24th	1 Mhdn to hospital.	
	" 25th	CAPT. E.W. SPURGIN wounded while in charge of Bde Dismtd men. 1 Jat to hospital. 2 Sikhs from hospital.	
	" 26th	Regt marched to MAMETZ 4.20 pm, arriving in bivouac at 6 pm. (8⅙ miles). 3 Jats & 1 Sikh to hospital.	

29th LANCERS

Army Form C. 2118.

WAR DIARY
or
INTELLIGENCE SUMMARY

September 1916 (Continued)

Instructions regarding War Diaries and Intelligence Summaries are contained in F. S. Regs., Part II, and the Staff Manual respectively. Title pages will be prepared in manuscript.

(Erase heading not required.)

Hour, Date, Place.	Summary of Events and Information	Remarks and references to Appendices.
MAMETZ September 27th	Regt marched to bivouac at BUSSY-LE-DAOURS (halting for 4 hours en route at old bivouac at SERRANCOURT) arriving at 5.30 PM (19 miles)	From 26th – 29th marches were all through very congested area which fact accounts for length of time taken on marches
BUSSY-LE-DAOURS " 28th	Regt marched to HANGEST-SUR-SOMME (billets) at 8.30 am arriving 12.20 PM (18½ miles).	
HANGEST-SUR-SOMME " 29th	Regt marched to BELLANCOURT (billets) at 8.10 AM arriving 12.15 PM. (12 miles)	
BELLANCOURT " 30th	Regt marched to MACHIEL (billets) at 8.5 am arriving 12.30 PM. (18 miles). (watering etc on the way).	
	1 Jat to hospl. 1 Jat from hospl. 1 Jat jd from Base.	
	During the month 48 horses were evacuated and 31 were received.	
	Paul Sumpter Lt Col comdg 29th Lancers	

Army Form C. 2118.

WAR DIARY
INTELLIGENCE SUMMARY
(Erase heading not required.)

29th LANCERS

OCTOBER. 1916.

Place	Date	Hour	Summary of Events and Information	Remarks and references to Appendices
MACHIEL	1/10		Distribution of Regiment as follows:- Hd Qrs. 9. 13 sqdns at MACHIEL C.D. Transport and 1 attached M.G sec at CAUMARTIN.	
"	2/10		1 Jat to Hospl.	
"	4/10		2 Jats and 1 Sikh to Hospl.	
"	5/10		2 Jats rejd from Hospl.	
"	10/10		1 Mussulman to Hospl.	
"	11/10		1 Jat to hospl.	
"	12/10		1 Jat to hospl.	
"	13/10		1 Jat and 2 Sikhs to hospl. 1 Sikh from Hospl.	
"	14/10		8 Jats came from Base.	
"	15/10		1 Jat to hospl. 1 Sikh from hospl. LT R.L.W. HERRICK to hospl.	During this period schemes with troops – Divisional Exercises, Brigade exercises + Regimental and Sqn exercises daily.
"	17/10		LT L.C. CLARKE to hospl. 1 bateman to hospl. 1 Jat from hospl.	
"	21/10		1 Jat to hospl. 1 Match R.H.A Driver to hospl.	
"	22/10		2 Jats to hospl. 3 Sikhs from Base.	

Army Form C. 2118.

WAR DIARY
INTELLIGENCE SUMMARY
(Erase heading not required)

29th LANCERS

OCTOBER 1916.

Instructions regarding War Diaries and Intelligence Summaries are contained in F. S. Regs., Part II. and the Staff Manual respectively. Title Pages will be prepared in manuscript.

Place	Date	Hour	Summary of Events and Information	Remarks and references to Appendices
MACHIEL	24/10		2 Tabs and 1 Batman to hospital.	
	25/10		2/Lt L.C. CLARKE rejd from hospital	
	26/10		2/Lt H.C. BELL rejd from Base (and rid posted to C sqdn) 1 Mhdn to hospl.	
	27/10		1 Sikh and 1 Jat to hospl. Lt R.L.W. MERRICK rejd from hospl.	
	28/10		1 Sikh to hospl. Working party of 1 BO (2/Lt CLARKE). 1 BOR. 1 JO. (Jem DAYA SINGH) and 30 I.O.R. & 1 Cook were posted to 13th Corps Area. (Reserve Army). Divisional party (300 men) commanded by MAJOR V.K.BIRCH.	During this period tactical exercises for Squadrons daily. Weather wet. Ground too soft for movement of large bodies across country without damaging fields and crops.
	30/10		1 Sikh to hospital 3 Sikhs 2 Jat's (farriers) } from Base 1 Jat from hospital.	
	31/10		1 Jat to hospital. During the month 12 horses evacuated (riding) 28 riding and 3 pack arrived from Base 2 riding rejd from M.V.S.	

Pares Sandgate Lt Colonel
Cmdg 29th Lancers.

Army Form C. 2118.

WAR DIARY
INTELLIGENCE SUMMARY
(Erase heading not required.)

29th Lancers

NOVEMBER 1916.

Instructions regarding War Diaries and Intelligence Summaries are contained in F. S. Regs., Part II. and the Staff Manual respectively. Title Pages will be prepared in manuscript.

Place	Date	Hour	Summary of Events and Information	Remarks and references to Appendices
MACHIEL	Nov 1st		1 Jat jd from hospl.	
"	2nd		Marched to new billetting area - arrived CHEPY on 11.50 A.M. distance 19 miles. Regiment distributed as follows:- H.Q. A.B.D. sqdns at CHEPY. C sqdn at PLATEUX attached M.G. sqdn lines at MONCHAUX.	
CHEPY	3rd		1 Jat to Hospl.	
	4th		1 Mdn from Hospl. No 1765 A.L. Dft DALIP SINGH (Dafdr.29L) wounded by shell fire.	
	5th		1 sikh } jd from Base. 2 Jats }	
	6th		1 Jat to Hospl.	
	9th		Jemadar GULAB SINGH to Hospl.	
	11th		Attached M.G. sqdn personnel moved from MONCHAUX to FRIERES and ZOTEUX. Working party under MAJOR BIRCH consisting of LT. J.C. CLARKE, JEMADAR DAYA SINGH 29 I.O.R and 1 follower rejoined by train and lorry (11.45 pm).	
	12th		1 Jat to Hospl. 4 Jats } from Base. 1 R.H.A driver }	
	15th		Jemadar DAYA SINGH to Hospl. 1 Sikh to Hospl.	
	16th		1 Sikh to Hospl.	
	17th		Jemadar GULAB SINGH rejd from Hospl. 9 I.O.R rejoined from Bde Signal Troop.	

2449 Wt. W14957/M90 750,000 1/16 J.B.C. & A. Forms/C.2118/12.

Army Form C. 2118.

WAR DIARY
or
INTELLIGENCE SUMMARY

(Erase heading not required.)

29th LANCERS. NOVEMBER 1916.

Place	Date	Hour	Summary of Events and Information	Remarks and references to Appendices
CHEDY	21st/16		To hospl 1 Sikh. Pioneer Corp of Pioneer Buttn left for work with Jem SAJA SINGH. BANZAI CORPS - (6 B/s. 6 Dfr. 5 J/s. 25 J.S.R) & followers.	
"	22nd		50 I.O.R {17 Mahrs from Base. Indication received that Lt R.A. RICE I.A.R invalided Corhile on leave in ENGLAND. {33 Jats	
"	23rd		To hospl 1 Jat From hospl 1 Sikh	
"	24th		2 ASC farriers to Base. From hospl 1 Jat.	
"	25th		To Base 50 I.O.R {10 Mahrs {40 Jats From C.I.H. 7 Rangars (I.O.R) joined.	
"	27th		No 2867 Sowar HABSARUP SINGH killed accidentally while with Pioneer Buttn. To hospl 1 Jat. Lt E.N.W. JOHNSTON I.A.R. aptd from Army Signal Service	
"	28th		To M.V.S. 1 I.O.R. (mule). During the month 3 horses evacuated and 1 horse shot. 6 horses rejd. A.K. Birch Major Commdg 29th Lancers	

Army Form C. 2118.

WAR DIARY
or
INTELLIGENCE SUMMARY
(Erase heading not required.)

29th LANCERS

DECEMBER, 1916.

Instructions regarding War Diaries and Intelligence Summaries are contained in F. S. Regs., Part II. and the Staff Manual respectively. Title Pages, will be prepared in manuscript.

Place	Date	Hour	Summary of Events and Information	Remarks and references to Appendices
CHEPY	2/12/16		1 Jat to Hospt. 1 Sikh from Hospt.	
	7/12/16		1 Indian to Hospt. LT. A.M. COLLETT. I.A.R joined Regt from Base LT. E.L. GAVANAGH. I.A.R do.	
	8/12/16		Rissaldar Major GHULAM DASTAGIR KHAN Jemadar ARBAB KHAN (27 L.C) } left invalid for return to INDIA. 1 Jat to hospt.	
	10/12/16		1 Jat to hospt.	
	12/12/16		LT COL P.B.SANGSTER D.S.O reported by medical Board in ENGLAND as unfit to return.	
	14/12/16		2 Jats rejoined from hospital. 4 B.Os, 11 B.O.R, 5 I.O.R, 100 I.O.R, 6 followers went to relieve an equal number of the Pioneer Batt'n at MONTAUBAN. Relieved Party rejoining Reg. at 5 p.m. Dfr AFZUL ALI proceed to ROUEN - as Instructor. Dfr RISAL SINGH " to Av.y Sig. School.	
	15/12/16 16/12/16		Lt R.O. BRADLEY and Lt (B.O.R. proceeded to ROUEN as Instructors. 1 Mess from hosp.	
	19/12/16		1 Jat to Hospt.	

2449 Wt. W14957/Mg0 750,000 1/16 J.B.C. & A. Forms/C.2118/12.

WAR DIARY
or
INTELLIGENCE SUMMARY

(Erase heading not required.)

Army Form C. 2118.

Decr 1916.

Place	Date	Hour	Summary of Events and Information	Remarks and references to Appendices
CHEPY	19.12.16		Captain Z.G. BURMESTER evacuated to hospital (sick).	
	22.12.16		No. 2928 Sr "GODHAR SINGH and No. 2619 Sr SANTA SINGH wounded with Pioneer Bath".	
	22.12.16		1 Mussalman to hospital	
	23.12.16		ditto "	
	24.12.16		Jr R.A. RICE IAR rejoined from Sick Leave.	
	26.12.16		1 Mussalman to hospital.	
	28.12.16		Major G.W. HEMANS rejoined from 38th Div. Sig. Coy.	
	30.12.16		1 Mussalman from hosp^t.	
	31.12.16		Major G. MARCHANT rejoined from 14th Corps.	
			11 horses evacuated during the month.	
			1 horse rejoined from M.V.S. during the month.	

C.K. Nosh Major
Comg. 29th Lancers.

www.ingramcontent.com/pod-product-compliance
Lightning Source LLC
Chambersburg PA
CBHW081547160426
43191CB00011B/1858